BUILDING AND DETAILING

SCALE MODEL
MUSCLE CARS

George S. Bojaciuk

KALMBACH
BOOKS

Printed in Canada

98 99 00 01 02 03 04 05 06   9 8 7 6 5 4 3 2 1

For more information, visit our website at http://www.kalmbach.com

Publisher's Cataloging-in-Publication
(Provided by Quality Books, Inc.)

Bojaciuk, George.
    Building and detailing scale model muscle cars / George
Bojaciuk. — 1st ed.
    p. cm.
    ISBN: 0-89024-566-5

    1. Muscle cars—Models—Design and construction.
I. Title.

TL240.B65 1998   629.22'12
                                   QBI97-41596

Book and cover design: Kristi Ludwig

ACKNOWLEDGMENTS

I've been modeling since I was old enough to hold a tube of glue, which was somewhere during Dwight D. Eisenhower's presidency. Over the years I have made many friends through the hobby, and these friends influenced my building techniques by the things they taught me. I've also tormented a host of hobby shop owners during my building career with my endless questions and requests. To say thanks to all these folks individually would probably fill a book in itself, and I would probably miss someone in the process anyhow. I would like to specifically mention the following model clubs that played an important role in polishing my building skills over the years through their informative meetings, NNL events, and the friendship the members offered me: Silent Traffic, Tri-State, MAMAs boys, and Northcoast Automotive Modelers. I would also like to acknowledge *Scale Auto Enthusiast, Car Modeler, Plastic Fanatic,* and *FineScale Modeler* magazines for giving me the forum in which to present my memories and models. A special thanks to my "basement buddies," Tom Buesgen and Karl Sheffer, for the hours of unadulterated fun spent kitbashing, painting, and concocting new projects.

CONTENTS

This book is dedicated to the memory of my dad, who taught me how to care for and appreciate cars; and to my wife, Debbie, whose love and support made this book possible.

FOREWORD

I've been writing articles and columns for more than 10 years now and have enjoyed working on each one. I have always tried to write my articles so that modelers at any experience level could read the piece and proceed to build a featured model. It would always give me great pleasure to attend a show and see someone who attempted a project I had written about. Not only did I see novice builders try something new, but I've seen seasoned veterans take my project to the next level of detail.

This book is designed to be a bench-top reference, featuring wiring diagrams, polishing techniques, building techniques, and my personal source guide for parts and conversion kits. My goal is to get you to try something new and different with each model you build. All you have to do is try one new technique with each model. Eventually, the combination of techniques may win you an award at a contest or NNL-type event. Ultimately, the book is designed to provide you hours of enjoyment. Good luck, and have fun!

Editor's note: Many of the chapters in this book appeared previously over the years as articles in *Scale Auto Enthusiast* and *FineScale Modeler* magazines.

1

THE HUMBLER

RESTORING AN ORIGINAL 1970 MPC PONTIAC GTO

"Humbler" was the name given to the 1970 Pontiac GTO. It was meant to humble the competition with its four engine options: the 400 cubic inch, two RAM AIRs, and—for the first time in a GM intermediate—a 455-cubic-inch mill. This GTO was heavier than Pontiac's previous offerings, with creature comforts like air conditioning, stereo, and custom interior appointments.

I can recall my first experience driving a white 1970 GTO

ENGINES

Standard—400 cubic inch—350 hp.
L74—400 cubic inch—Ram Air III—366 hp.
L67—400 cubic inch—Ram Air IV—370 hp.
L75—455 cubic inch—360 hp. Note: Ram Air induction was offered with this engine option.

TRANSMISSIONS

Three-speed manual
Four-speed manual
Turbo Hydra-Matic

EXTERIOR COLORS AND CODES

Starlight Black	19 (A)
Palomino Copper	63 (B)
Polar White	10 (C)
Bermuda Blue	25 (D)
Atoll Blue	28 (E)
Lucerne Blue	26 (F)
Baja Gold	55 (G)
Palisade Green	45 (H)
Castillian Bronze	67 (J)
Mint Turquoise	34 (K)
Keylime Green	43 (L)
Pepper Green	48 (M)
Burgundy	78 (N)
Palladium Silver	14 (P)
Verdoro Green	47 (Q)
Cardinal Red	75 (R)
Coronado Gold	53 (S)
Orbit Orange	60 (T)
Carousel Red	65 (V)
Goldenrod Yellow	51 (W)
Sierra Yellow	50 (Y)
Granada Gold	58 (Z)

CONVERTIBLE TOP COLORS AND CODES

White	1
Black	2
Sandalwood	5
Dark Gold	7

CORDOVA VINYL TOP COLORS AND CODES

White	1
Black	2
Sandalwood	5
Dark Gold	7
Dark Green	9

INTERIOR COLORS

Blue
Saddle
Green
Sandalwood
Black
Red

455. There was a certain thrill when I slipped the key into the ignition and turned over the 360 horses. As the engine came alive, the gauges jumped nervously—just waiting to record the ride of a lifetime. I turned the car onto the open road and stepped into the accelerator. The feel of torque and horsepower pushing me into the seat was what "muscle" is all about!

The memory of this particular GTO still lives, and the excitement returns every time I look on my display shelf. In 1970, MPC captured the moment in plastic. Unfortunately, because of my inexperience and poor taste, I captured the moment in horror. I built the GTO with the drag option and painted it with Krylon navy blue. Of course, the paint was incompatible with the plastic, so the car took on a textured look because of the plastic crazing. I eventually repainted the model four more times, retaining the drag option. It was doomed for the scrap box.

Several years later my interest in modeling resurfaced seriously, and I went out in search of another "Goat." I was shocked to find out how much a replacement, original kit was worth—promos were priced even higher. Restoring my original kit seemed to be the logical option. The 1970 GTO was reissued sometime in the early 1990s.

I carefully disassembled he model using a no. 11 X-acto blade. Fortunately, the glue had dried, so disassembly was quite easy. The chrome pieces virtually lifted out, since in my earlier days I never scraped chrome prior to gluing. I lowered the heavily painted body into Amway's Industro Clean for several weeks of soaking. I've had good results with this product. You can easily reuse it by pouring

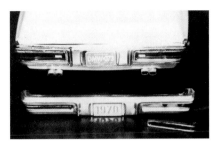

The original bumper was worn in spots, and the taillights were broken. The 1972 GTO kit supplied a new bumper and taillights. I cut aluminum tubing and recessed it into the valance panel to achieve exhaust detail.

it back into the bottle through a coffee filter. This product became difficult to find after a while and I currently use Simple Green, which will lift the paint in a few days. Simple Green is also environmentally friendly and can be disposed of safely. While the car body soaked, I researched the real car in car magazines, repair manuals, sales brochures, and books. This was also a good time to assess the reusability of the kit parts. You may need to locate replacement sources for parts that are beyond help. In my case, MPC helped a great deal with the then-reissued 1972 GTO. All the parts I needed were in one box: a new chassis, interior glass, GTO 455 decals, and—most important—a new chrome rear bumper. A good working knowledge of parts interchangeability will save you money and time when hunting down parts. Repair manuals supply information on chassis and model year similarities.

The original and reissued engines appeared diminutive in the vast engine compartment. I detailed and used a 455 engine from a later MPC Trans Am kit, since it looked better in the engine bay. I retained the original valve covers. I painted the block with Testor's Model Master

The condition and appearance of the original wheels were poor. With a few detailing tricks and the addition of deeper trim rings, I brought the drab wheels back to life. You can add rim rings to any wheel for a deep-dish look.

Pontiac engine blue. The original chassis was beyond repair, so I scrapped it in favor of a new one. I opened up two holes near the gas tank to accommodate the mounting screws. I painted the chassis flat black, with the frame rails accented in gloss black. The only modification I made to the rear suspension was slight trimming and adding watch post shocks and small coil springs I found in an automotive spring assortment pack.

The wheels and tires needed special consideration and detail. The original Rally II wheels were, to say the least, pitiful. But with my tire choice, I needed something with a deep-dish look. After some thought, I derived a solution quite by accident. I detailed the wheels with flat black and a red center cap. Adding a chrome trim ring that I found in a parts box funny car kit gave the depth I desired for a deep-dish look.

I used a new interior from the 1972 kit and detailed it using a 000 brush and chrome silver paint. I also applied woodgrain where appropriate. The 1970 and 1972 interiors were identical.

I readied the body for prep and priming. I sanded it smooth with no. 400 grit sandpaper and primed it with automotive gray

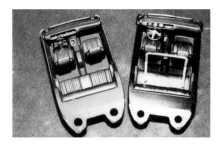

I could have refinished the old interior (right)—but why bother? I detailed the new interior with a 000 brush and chrome silver paint, applying woodgrain where appropriate.

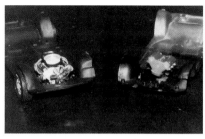

The stock engine appeared diminutive in the chassis (right). I detailed a scrap box engine and lowered it into a new chassis.

At one time I had hot-knifed the old chassis to accept a Chevy 454 tunnel ram engine. I replaced the chassis with a new one. The only modification I needed to make was to open the screw mounting holes near the fuel tank.

I special-ordered the RAM AIR induction system cast in resin.

primer. Unfortunately, the plastic crazed again. Obviously, the plastic would prove to be incompatible with automotive paints. I then resanded and reprimed the body with Testor's flat white and finished with Testor's Model Master classic white.

After the body had dried for several weeks, I detailed it. I applied adhesive-backed foil, then did other detailing with Tamiya's silver paint marker. I found this marker quick and easy to use, but offer a word of caution: Practice control, otherwise you will have a mess.

I applied the marker lights and gloss-coated the entire body. I painted the area between the grille and chrome surround with flat aluminum, to match infor-

mation I found in the sales brochure. I replaced the rear bumper with a new one from the 1972 kit and detailed it. I made quad exhaust tips from 1/8″ aluminum tubing and recessed it into the rear valance panel. Then I installed new glass and mated the body, interior, and chassis. I also added radiator hoses, heater hoses, and other engine details. The restoration was complete!

Besides building the standard GTO, you can also convert this MPC kit into a Judge.

The Judge had blacked-out grilles and grille surrounds. A black spoiler was installed under the front valance, but not on all cars. One could order the rear spoiler painted to match the body color or matte black; some spoilers had a small stripe on each side. Factory combinations for color and stripe combinations could be superseded by customer preference. The "eyebrow" decals over the wheel wells were part of the package (RPO 422),

but early cars had the 1969 stripes. You can find these stripes in the Monogram 1969 GTO Judge kit. In addition, any GTO model could have Judge striping, but this alone did not make it a Judge. Decals behind the front wheel openings on the right-hand side of the deck lid said "THE JUDGE," and the lower right-hand side of the glove box door had a special nameplate. The scoop openings on the hood were painted matte black. Manual shift models came with a Hurst T-handle shifter. Available engines included the RAM AIR III standard and the L67 RAM AIR IV, and late in the model year the 455 could be special-ordered.

The suspension was the same as any with GTO. The standard tires were G70 x 14 black walls; however, white-lettered tires and white walls were also available. The dechromed Rally II wheels were part of the package, but a buyer could choose the optional trim rings. "Judge" decals are available from Fred Cady Design.

You can restore many older kits using current kits and good reference materials. With this and some careful planning, you can turn any one of those junk cars into something worth displaying.

Judge Color and Stripe Combinations

Yellow decal and stripes
63, 55, 45, 48, 47, 50, 58

Black decal and stripes
78, 75

Orange decal and stripes
25, 28, 34, 60

Blue decal and stripes
19, 10, 14

2
SPECIAL-ORDER SUPERCAR

BUILDING A 1969 YENKO CAMARO

In 1969, you could walk into any Chevy dealership and actually order a race car. At Yenko Sportscars in Cannonsburg, Pennsylvania, your order was extra special. The Yenko S/C Camaro was based on the factory L-72 package and came equipped with a 427-cubic-inch engine rated by NHRA and the Yenko sales brochure at 450 hp. Yenko produced 201 Camaros, removing the pollution controls and adding headers and special graphics. The L-72 Camaro was actually a base Z/28 with all the standard Z options. Yenko added other features like a 140 mph speedometer, front and rear spoilers, functional air induction hood, a dash-mounted tachometer, and extra gauges. You could order a Yenko Camaro with either a

Muncie M21 four-speed with Hurst linkage, or with an automatic with an optional Hurst Dual-Gate shifter. The automatic cars were equipped with the milder, hydraulic-cammed 410 hp engine; this version is very rare today. Were they fast? Quarter-mile times of 11.5 to 12.0 seconds were a reality.

I experienced my first Yenko in 1977. Words cannot describe the feeling I got when I was thrown back into the seat, with the throttle open and the tires smoking. Going through the gears was pure excitement. I have attempted to recreate that feeling by building a scale replica of one of my favorite muscle cars.

Before beginning any project, you need to do tedious research. Dealer brochures, mag-

azines, photos, and letters to "experts" helped me reproduce an accurate model. I first wrote an article about this project in 1986, and at that time only one article had been written about detailing Yenko Camaros. Vince Emme, the resident Yenko expert responsible for documenting these rare cars, contributed to that lone article. I wrote to Vince, who graciously provided the information and detailed pictures I needed to complete the project.

I used Monogram's 1969 Camaro Z/28 kit as the base for my project. At that time it was the only kit available for a 1969 Camaro. Revell released the Yenko Camaro kit no. 7132 several years after I published the story of this conversion. Coincidentally, the box art showed a

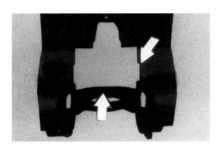

I needed to modify the chassis only slightly: I removed the engine mounting tabs and notched each side for exhaust clearance.

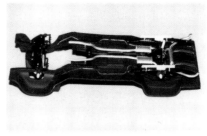

An exhaust system, from the parts box, fit with only minor trimming.

I detailed the 427 engine with ignition wires, hoses, correct air cleaner assembly, and an engine displacement decal.

yellow car, just like my model! I was told that my conversion prompted the kit's production, although Revell never sent me a letter stating this. I like to think that my model had such an influence. Fred Cady supplied the beautiful graphics for the original model, and the parts box supplied the rest.

The wheels were the biggest challenge, since I chose to equip the model with Chevy Rally wheels. My original plan was to use MPC wheels mated to AMT's L60-15 tires. But 1/25 scale is not quite 1/24 scale, so the tire combination did not look right during preliminary test fitting. The tires looked more like F70s than the desired L60s, and other wheel selections from the parts box

detracted from the authentic appearance of the Yenko. American Racing Wheels—specifically the Torque-thrust—were a correct option, and I found a good set in Monogram's 1968 GTO kit. Unfortunately, I had to make the Rally wheels.

I found the parts I needed to make the Rally wheels in AMT's 1969 Chevelle kit: four center caps and four wheel assemblies. I made trim rings from four Star mags found in the parts box; two of the mags are included in the Monogram Camaro kit. I cut out the centers and achieved the proper amount of offset by sanding 1/16″ from the bottom. I also sanded the wheel assembly from the AMT kit 1/8″, reducing the offset even more. I detailed the

wheels, mated them to the trim ring, and added the center cap. Initially I had planned to use Monogram's Goodyear Rally GT tires, but changed my mind when I found a set of Otaki B.F. Goodrich Radial T/As. I detailed the raised letters with Tamiya flat white, XF-2.

I pirated a big-block Chevy engine from Monogram's 1970 Malibu kit. I made a cold air induction box by modifying an air cleaner from Monogram's 1970 Mustang Boss 429. I removed the snorkel and air cleaner element and replaced it with appropriate Chevy pieces from the parts box. This assembly is now available in resin from Muscle in Miniature. I painted the engine block with Testor's Chevy engine orange enamel and detailed it with ignition wires, radiator hoses, and an air cleaner decal, using pictures from car magazines for placement guidance. I used stock exhaust manifold from the Malibu kit, along with a conventional under-the-car exhaust system salvaged from AMT's 1971 Nova SS kit.

The chassis needed only minor modification to accommodate the 427 engine. I removed tabs on the engine crossmember and notched the frame rails for exhaust system clearance. No other modifications were necessary. I sprayed Testor's flat black on the floor pan and accented the frame rails with gloss black. Chassis engraving lent itself to paint detailing, which I accomplished using a fine-tip silver paint marker and a steady hand.

I sprayed the interior flat black and detailed it with a 000 brush and Testor's silver enamel, using a dealer brochure as a reference for application of the woodgrain accents. The kit interior had one major disappoint-

I detailed the interior according to a dealer brochure, taking interior parts from various kits.

I removed all of the Z/28 emblems and 302 hood emblems.

The grille is actually two grilles cut near the center, then sanded and glued. The seam is almost invisible.

ment—the seats. The Recaro-type front seats had no seat backs, which made them look unfinished, and the back seat was missing altogether. I used 1970 Malibu bucket seats along with the steering column and the steering wheel. This still left the problem of no back seat; I found one quite by accident in the parts box. A rear seat from AMT's 1971 Nova SS kit fit without any modification, and the seat pattern was even a close match to the front buckets. I finished off the interior by adding a Hurst shifter and a Stewart-Warner tachometer.

I removed all of the molded-on Z/28 emblems, 302 hood emblems, and hood pins from the body prior to spraying with Testor's gull gray primer. Yenko Camaros were available in six factory colors: Hugger Orange (72), Daytona Yellow (76), Fathom Green (57), Rally Green (79), LeMans Blue (71), and Olympic Gold (65). A black vinyl top also could be ordered. I selected Daytona Yellow acrylic lacquer for my project car and airbrushed it with several light coats. For the nonpurist or someone who doesn't own an airbrush, Testor's chrome yellow sprayed over a flat white primer will give a close match. After sufficient drying time, I covered all

the window trim with Bare Metal foil and added black accents to the lower rocker panels and to the area between the rear taillights. I used magazine articles and photos to guide my placing the Fred Cady decals, which were applied according to their instructions. I taped off the hood with 3-M Mylar tape in the design pictured and sprayed it black, then used dry transfer decals to duplicate the "sYc" on the hood. Newer versions of Fred Cady's decal sheet contain all the decals needed, as does the Revell kit. When it was dry, I sprayed the body with two coats of Testor's Glosscote.

Initially, the Z/28 grille emblem had been scraped out and painted flat black. Unfortunately, it looked as if it had been scraped out and painted! Furthermore, a Yenko grille is silver, not black. I cut two grilles in

A photo of the hood graphics provided the detail that the Fred Cady decals started.

half and joined the two nonemblemed halves. I made the cut just past the center mark and carefully sanded and cemented the parts. Then I painted the grille flat black and wiped it with thinner to bring out the silver raised portions.

I made the front spoiler from sheet plastic, painted it black, and attached it to the front valance pan. I fitted and installed the grille, bumpers, taillights and interior glass in the interior and chassis. Then I installed the tires and wheels, and the car was complete.

The thrill and excitement of that ride in 1977 was rekindled when I recreated this piece of muscle car history in scale. The real Yenko S/C Camaro may be a rare collector's piece, but anyone can have this model muscle car with a minimal amount of effort.

Muscle in Miniature offers the Yenko air cleaner in resin, if you choose not to use the Revell kit.

3
HIDDEN HEADLIGHTS

BUILDING A PAIR OF GTOS

The body style of the 1968 and 1969 GTOs has always been my favorite. I've tried to capture the feeling of both GTOs in scale: the 1968 Verdoro Green 400 and the showroom-new Judge. I needed two Monogram kits, the 1968 GTO Street Machine and the 1969 GTO Judge kit, both by Monogram, to build both of these replicas. At the time of this conversion, both kits were readily available. The 1968 kit was only released once and has become difficult to obtain. Scale Resin Detailers offers a 1968 GTO conversion kit in resin.

The 1968 GTO 400

The 1969 GTO 400 was Motor Trend's 1968 Car of the Year, and it sold more than 900,000 units—a first for Pontiac. The body lines were clean, smooth, and flowing. The car sported the new Endura front bumper, which added considerably to the clean lines, although you could order a GTO with a chrome bumper. Stick-shift cars received chrome exhaust extensions. A factory first was the addition of identification decals,

found on the rear quarters. GTOs were also available with or without hidden headlights. Four optional engines were offered in addition to the standard four-barrel, 350 hp, 400-cubic-inch engine:

• 400 cubic inch, two barrel, 265 hp
• 400 HO cubic inch, four barrel, 360 hp
• 400 cubic inch, Ram Air, four barrel, 360 hp
• 400 cubic inch, Ram Air II, four barrel, 370 hp (available after April 1, 1968, to replace the Ram Air)

Ram Air engines were mated to Turbo Hydra-matic or the M21, close ratio four speed. The only rear ratio was 4.33:1 with mandatory Safe-T-Track, limited slip differential. Transmissions available included a three-speed manual, four-speed manual, and automatic with Hurst Dual Gate shifter.

You will need two Monogram GTO kits to build the model conversion: The 1968 GTO Street Machine and the 1969 GTO Judge kit. If the 1968 kit is difficult to

obtain, you can purchase a 1968 conversion kit from Scale Resin Detailers. You will need the hood, the carburetor, and the air cleaner from the 1969 kit. Note that my replica is not 100 percent correct. Missing details include the round outside rearview mirrors, vent windows, the crest on top of the front bumper, the 1968 side marker lights, the correct interior seat pattern, and the "GTO" on the trunk lid.

The kit 1968 GTO body is actually a 1969, so it needed some work. I removed the molded-on GTO emblems on the front fenders with a hobby file and smoothed the area with 600 grit sandpaper. I made a GTO triangle crest by pressing aluminum foil onto an emblem from a MPC 1967 GTO body. I filled the back of the impression with five-minute epoxy and trimmed the foil after the epoxy was dry. Then I glued the emblem in place on the front fender. I made the 400 emblems in the same manner, using a MPC Firebird 400 hood as the master. Then I primed the body with Testor's Model Master primer.

12

1968 GTO
Exterior Colors and Codes

Starlight Black	A
Cameo Ivory	C
Alpine Blue	D
Aegean Blue	E
Nordic Blue	F
April Gold	G
Autumn Bronze	I
Meridian Turquoise	K
Aleutian Blue	L
Flambeau Burgundy	N
Springmist Green	P
Verdoro Green	Q
Solar Red	R
Primavera Beige	T
Nightshade Green	V
Mayfair Maize	Y

Interior Colors and Codes

Teal	219
Turquoise	220
Gold	221
Black	223
Parchment	224
Red	225

Convertible Top Colors and Codes

White	1
Black	2
Teal	5
Gold	8

Vinyl Top Colors and Codes

Ivory	1
Black	2
Teal	5
Gold	6 (8)

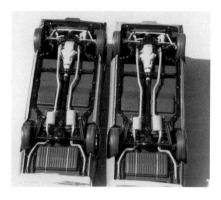

The chassis detail is identical for both models.

To make the emblems for the 1968, I found a body with the appropriate markings. I pressed aluminum foil onto the emblem and made a copy. Then I filled the back depression in the foil with epoxy and let it dry. After trimming the emblem, I glued it to the body.

At $10.00 a pint in 1986, I had to find a suitable substitute for Verdoro Green paint. I found that Duplicolor's 1971 Chrysler Sherwood Green, when sprayed over the primer, was a close match and readily available. Today Model Car World offers automotive paints in small quantities and at reasonable prices. When the paint was dry, I detailed the moldings using Bare Metal foil and Testor's Model Master chrome silver paint. I glued the emblems to the rocker panels directly behind the front wheel openings. I detailed the GTO crest and the 400 emblems with Testor's Model Master red marker light paint. Then I sprayed the entire body with Testor's Glosscote.

Since the 1968 hood was cut out for carburetor clearance, I used the 1969 kit hood. If you prefer a 1968 Ram Air option, you can modify the air cleaner assembly from Revell's 1969 Yenko Camaro, kit no. 7132, to fit. You would need to remove the snorkel snout from the air cleaner assembly and shape the hood underside piece to fit. Muscle in Miniature also offers this assembly in resin.

I built the engine box stock from the 1969 kit and detailed it with wires, hoses, fuel lines, and a removable air cleaner. I painted the engine block with Testor's Model Master Pontiac engine blue. I also built the chassis box stock, painting it flat black with gloss black frame rails. I painted the exhaust and steering linkage with Testor's Model Master steel. The interior is actually a 1969 interior and was built box stock; I used 1969 GTO dealer literature for reference. I also paint-detailed

the wheels as shown in the dealer brochure and detailed the tires to resemble "redlines." I sanded the tire tread for added realism.

I detailed the 1968 kit's vent windows with silver paint. When I added them to the car they looked out of place, so I decided not to use them. At some later date I may add these vent windows using Evergreen strip plastic and clear acetate. Finally, I detailed the front grille with flat black and the taillights with Testor's red marker light paint. You may or may not add GTO decals to the rear quarters; I added them with dry transfer decals.

The 1969 Ram Air IV Judge

The Judge was introduced as a top-of-the-line model in January 1969. As standard equipment, the Judge was equipped with a 400-cubic-inch Ram Air V-8 rated at 366 hp, dual exhausts, a three-speed transmission and floor-mounted shifter with a Hurst T-Handle, and a 3.55:1 rear end ratio. A rear deck spoiler, G70 x 14 blackwall tires, and Rally II wheels without trim rings completed the package. Options included various rear axle ratios, a hood-mounted tachometer, a Rally gauge package, and a Ram

1969 GTO
Exterior Colors and Codes

Starlight Black	(10)	A
Expresso Brown	(61)	B
Cameo White	(50)	C
Warwick Blue	(53)	D
Liberty Blue	(51)	E
Windward Blue	(87)	F
Antique Gold	(65)	G
Limelight Green	(59)	H
Castillian Bronze	(89)	J
Crystal Turquoise	(55)	K
Claret Red	(86)	L
Midnight Green	(57)	M
Burgundy	(67)	N
Palladium Silver	(69)	P
Verdoro Green	(73)	Q
Matador Red	(52)	R
Champagne	(63)	S
Carousel Red	(72)	T
Nocturne Blue	(88)	V
Goldenrod Yellow	(76)	W
Mayfair Maize	(40)	Y

Interior Colors and Codes

Blue	250
Gold	252
Red	254
Green	256
Parchment	257
Black	258

Convertible Top Colors and Codes

White	1
Black	2
Dark Blue	3
Dark Green	9

Vinyl Top Colors and Codes

Black	2
Dark Blue	3
Parchment	5
Dark Fawn	8
Dark Green	9

Air IV engine rated at 370 hp with functional scoops.

The first 5000 cars were painted Carousel Red, which

If you use very thin coats, you can apply automotive paint over Testor's primer.

Using the 1969 hood saves the time you would spend filling the hole in this 1968 kit hood.

really made the car stand out, but other factory colors were available. Proper car color and stripe combinations are described in a chart on this page.

Pontiac assembled the original Carousel Red Judges with red/blue/yellow stripes and decals. In February 1969, this stripe color scheme changed to black/red/yellow.

Along with the special striping, "THE JUDGE" was emblazoned on the front fender and the rear deck spoiler. The words also appeared on the glove box door. The Judge actually started as a joke, stemming from the 1960s TV show *Laugh-In*.

I built my replica Judge primarily out-of-the-box with only a few changes and additions. I added a Ram Air tub to the detailed engine compartment, which included hoses, wires, and air cleaner. A Fred Cady decal sheet supplied a "RAM AIR IV" decal, which I added to each side of the twin hood scoops.

I built and detailed the interior and chassis as described for the 1968 GTO, and I used the kit tires but reversed them for the black wall look. I stripped the chrome from the Rally II wheels and sprayed them with Testor's Model Master steel, then overcoated with Testor's Dullcote and detailed them as previously described.

I painted the body Carousel Red using an airbrush. Testor's Model Master Chevrolet engine orange was an exact match to the GTO color, which I confirmed with a Pontiac dealer color chart for 1969. After painting the car, I applied a "kiss-coat" of thinner and the remaining film of paint in the jar to give the body a gloss smooth finish. To do this, empty the airbrush paint jar and fill it with thinner to give the appearance of a tinted thinner. Spray a very light coat over the entire body while the paint is still wet. Don't overdo this, or you'll have a runny mess—or worse yet, you'll lift paint off the body. Spray this "kiss-coat" only once and let it dry.

From that point, I finished the Judge in the same manner as the 1968. I added all the body details using magazine photos and dealer brochures as a guide.

1969 Judge Stripe/Body Color Combinations

White/yellow/green*
  59, 57, 73, 40

Yellow/red/blue*
  10, 50, 53, 51, 55, 69, 72

White/red/black*
  61, 65, 67, 52, 63

*Denotes key color

4

REQUIEM FOR A HEMI-WEIGHT

CONVERTING MONOGRAM'S 1971 SATELLITE INTO A HEMI-GTX

The Satellite was Plymouth's basic intermediate line in 1971. This included the Coupe, Road Runner, Custom, Sebring, Brougham, Regent, Sebring Plus, and GTX. The body was redesigned to incorporate a fuselage body style. The hood had two outboard-facing scoops that boasted engine sizes 340, 383, 440, 440 + 6, or Hemi. The Hemi was detuned in 1971 and the compression ratio was dropped to 10.2:1, but this still left it a brutal performer with 425 gross hp and 350 net hp. GTX power plants were the 440, the 440 six-pack, and the Hemi. Plymouth produced a total of 30 Hemi GTX models in 1971; 11 were four-speeds and 19 were Torque Flite automatics.

When Monogram introduced the Satellite kit no. 2213, I had to have one—not because it was a Satellite, but because of the body style! There was something appealing about the car and, other than an original issue kit, there was nothing else on the market at the time of Monogram's release. Revell released a 1971 GTX kit no. 7608 in 1995, which was an update of the Satellite kit with proper GTX upgrades and 440 six-pack engine option. This may be a better choice for a build-up because of kit availability and body modifications.

To build the Hemi GTX from the Satellite kit you will need one Monogram 1971 Hemicuda

kit no. 2292 or no. 2243 (originally I used a 'Cuda Street Machine kit no. 2701) and a 1970 GTX kit no. 2730. From these three kits you can also derive a 440 six-pack variation and a standard 440 single four-barrel option, four-speed and automatic versions, if you so desire. For the Hemi, the parts you will need from the 'Cuda kit are the Hemi engine, exhaust manifolds, and carbs. From the 1970 GTX, you'll need the chrome air cleaner and the shifter. If you want the Air Grabber option, use the Revell 1971 GTX.

I built the chassis box stock and painted it flat black with the frame rails accented in gloss black. I painted the exhaust system with Testor's Model Master steel and the mufflers with Testor's Model Master chrome silver.

I removed the exhaust tips and replaced them with 1/8″ aluminum tubing. I added a slight bevel to the end of the tubing that would stick out from under the bumper, then detailed it with red stripes to simulate the red vented tips shown in the dealer brochure. My kit came with a slightly warped chassis and an exhaust system that curved to the right. Both problems corrected themselves when the pieces were glued into their appropriate locations.

I scrapped the kit tires in favor of Otaki's Big and Little, B.F. Goodrich Radial T/As. I painted the side wall letters on the tires with Tamiya flat white—this method seems to work best with real rubber tires. If you're looking for added period realism, sand the treads on the tires until they are almost bald—most

Exterior Colors and Codes

Winchester Gray Metallic	GA4
Glacial Blue Metallic	GB2
True Blue Metallic	GB5
Evening Blue Metallic	GB7
Amber Sherwood Metallic	GF3
Sherwood Green Metallic	GF7
Autumn Bronze Metallic	GK6
Tunisian Tan Metallic	GT2
Snow White	GW3
Formal Black	TX9
Gold Leaf Metallic	GY8
Tawny Gold Metallic	GY9
Meadow Green	GJ3
Green Go	FJ6
Lemon Twist	FY1
Tor-Red	EV2
Plum Crazy	FC7
Butterscotch	EL5
Citron Yella	GY3

Interior Colors

Blue
Green
Tan
Gold
Gunmetal
Orange/Black
Black

Vinyl Top Colors

Black
White
Green
Gold

I retrieved the Hemi engine from the 'Cuda Street Machine kit and detailed it using car magazines as a reference.

I detailed the interior using a dealer brochure as a reference. The GTX was the top-of-the-line model, so there was plenty of wood trim.

Hemi cars of the 1970s era sported bald rear tires! I used the wheels from the kit and detailed them by painting the slots flat black and the wheel itself steel, leaving the impression of a chrome trim ring and center cap. This part is tedious but the end result is well worth it. The tire and wheel assembly should be left until final assembly to ensure proper fit, to ensure wheel spacing within the body lines, and to simplify chassis installation. When I test fitted the tires, I needed to raise the rear tire for clearance. I added a 1/8˝ piece of Plastruct box tubing to each side of the rear spring mounting pads. This was hidden from view by the rear valance panel when I glued the chassis to the body. The rear suspension risers in the Cuda Street Machine kit could also be used.

I painted the engine block orange and the exhaust manifolds gunmetal gray. I soaked the chromed air cleaner from the 1970 GTX kit in Mr. Clean for about an hour to remove the chrome. This really works well for removing chrome; however, it will not remove the clear part of the plating, and you should avoid using hot lacquers. When the dechromed part is ready, all you need to do is rinse the part in warm water and let it dry.

I detailed the air cleaner by painting it orange, adding white to the element area, placing a Hemi decal from Fred Cady on the lid, and painting the bottom seal semigloss black. I sanded the tops of the carbs to remove most of the air horn, then glued the air cleaner on top. This step ensured proper hood clearance. I drilled out the valve covers in the spark plug area and added wires from the distributor to the appropriate spark plug holes. Once I had completed the engine, I trimmed away a part of the exhaust system from the exhaust manifold. The amount to trim depends on the length of the exhaust pipe. This also could be left alone and you could trim the chassis pipe instead. The important thing is that the engine fits the engine compartment perfectly. A purist may want to move the transmission mount back a minimal amount. At this point I tied the exhaust manifolds into the chassis exhaust system.

I painted the interior with semigloss black and detailed it with woodgrain accents on the dash, gauge area, console, and door panels. Since the Hemi was mated to a four-speed transmission, I removed the automatic brake pedal and added a new brake and clutch pedal assembly from the parts box. I salvaged a four-speed shifter from the 1970 GTX kit and glued it over the automatic shift pattern on the console. If you desire an automatic transmission, the Satellite kit 440 engine has one molded to it. An automatic option can also be achieved by cutting away the trans and grafting it to the back of the Hemi. I detailed the four-speed shifter by painting the handle flat brown to simulate woodgrain and painting the shifter boot flat black to simulate rubber. I detailed the gauges with

I also detailed the Mopar Rallye wheels with the aid of a dealer brochure. I painted the slots flat black and the painted the wheel with steel. This gave the impression of a trim ring and a center cap.

I painted the chassis flat black with gloss black accents, then picked up other chassis detail with silver and steel paint.

silver paint, using a dry-brushing technique to bring out the raised numerals on the gauge faces.

The body was molded in black and I could have polished it out. My preference was to pay extra attention to the body because of the scratches and mold lines that it had. I removed the mold lines by the roof pillars as well as small amounts of body flash I found along the body creases. I then wet-sanded the body using 400 grit sandpaper, then 600 grit sanding film, and sprayed it with primer. I mixed Testor's Model Master classic black with thinner and sprayed it on with an airbrush. Here I encountered a problem: When I mixed the paint I used too much thinner, so when I applied it to the body some areas actually crazed. Then I stripped the paint from the body and prepped it again for painting. This time I used the proper mixture of thinner to paint, and I got more favorable results. I let the body fully dry for a week. This eliminates fingerprints that occur when handling the body if its finish coat is too soft.

I added Bare Metal foil to all the moldings and added GTX emblems to the rear quarter panels using white extended gothic decals. You can find a complete decal sheet of this type of lettering in hobby shops. Different

sizes were available on the same sheet so that the same effect can be achieved as on a real GTX. Be sure to use good reference pictures, as there were two GTX decals on the front of the lower rear quarter panel ahead of the rear wheel openings, one on each side. Note also the configuration of the GTX lettering: A smaller GTX decal appeared on the right-hand side of the trunk lid, and the kit's strobe decal was used over the roof. I detailed the hood using dry transfer lettering to spell Hemi, along with the kit strobe decals on either side of the scoops. I gloss coated the entire body to add depth to the jet-black finish. I made the GTX emblem in the grille using the foil and epoxy technique discussed in depth in Chapter 14. I glued the emblem in place after trimming, then painted the grille center flat black and brought out the highlights by buffing with a thinner-soaked paper towel.

I glued the interior glass, mirror, and interior compartment into the body. Then I

I made the GTX emblem with a foil and epoxy technique, then glued it to the center rib of the grille.

mated the body assembly with the chassis and engine assembly. With the engine now in the engine compartment, I could locate the radiator. I used the GTX radiator after removing 5/16˝ from the bottom, then glued it to the outside of the radiator support rather than to the inside of the engine compartment. I relocated the radiator cap from the center to a side of the radiator. The 'Cuda kit supplied the Hemi upper radiator hose, which now fit perfectly.

I detailed under the hood using Testor's Model Master chrome silver paint, flat white for the washer bottle and battery case, and flat black for the kit hoses. For a little extra detail, I added a "DIE HARD" decal to the side of the battery case. I installed front and rear bumpers and detailed the taillights using Testor's Model Master marker light red.

With the car almost finished, it was time to locate and glue the tire and wheel assemblies in place. I brought the rear tires to the edge of the fender lip, then glued them to the wheel back with epoxy. A rearview mirror on each door, a pair of license plates, and a bit of flat black paint on the inside of the exhaust tips completed the project.

I used Micro Scale decals for the graphics, combining sizes to achieve the desired look. A word of caution: These decals are ultra-thin, so keep plenty of decal set handy to untangle any problems.

5
THE DOCTOR'S PRESCRIPTION

BUILDING A 1970 OLDSMOBILE 442 W-30

The 1970 Olds 442 was an exciting car in its own right, but the W-30 package made it even more so. Dealer literature described the W-30 package as "Available in 442 coupes, convertible. Includes fiberglass hood with cold air hood scoops; dual hood pin locks; big Rally stripes on hood; plus body side stripes; two sport-styles outside mirrors (left-hand mirror with remote control); special "W" identification on front fenders; special 455 cube, cold air V-8 with 'select fit' of critical parts; performance calibrated 4-bbl cold air carburetor; low restriction air cleaner; lightweight aluminum manifold; high overlap cam; new single piston manual disc brakes up front with large drums in back; heavy duty cooling; new weight reducing body insulators; super wide G70 x 15 fiberglass belted black walls with raised white letters mounted on heavy duty 7˝ wheels; anti-spin performance axle. Not included in the W-30 package, but already standard in 442 are dual low-restriction exhausts and heavy duty FE-2 suspension with front and rear stabilizer bars."

Olds had a pretty impressive package, and the W-30 was a classy car to drive. Its 455-cubic-inch engine was rated at 370 hp, and the tires could be broken loose at 60 miles per hour. The torque was unreal—and it was torque that buried you into the seat. The automatic cars received a milder hydraulic cam that cut horsepower by 15 but actually made the car more drivable.

The 442 shown here was patterned after a car I saw in a magazine—one that I would not mind owning today.

A Johan 1970 Olds 442 kit was the basis for this conversion project, and I initially planned to scratchbuild the W-30 hood. So I put the project aside because of the complexity of building the hood. Then I found an ad in a model magazine's classified sec-

Exterior Colors and Codes

Porcelain White	10
Platinum	14
Ebony Black	19
Azure Blue	20
Astro Blue	25
Twilight Blue	28
Reef Turquoise	34
Aegean Aqua	38
Aspen Green	45
Sherwood Green	48
Bamboo	50
Sebring Yellow	51
Nugget Gold	53
Galleon Gold	55
Burnished Gold	58
Copper	63
Rally Red	73
Matador Red	75
Burgundy Mist	78

Interior Colors

Black
Ivory
Blue
Green
Saddle
Gold

Vinyl Top Colors

Black
White
Blue
Green
Gold
Saddle

Convertible Top Colors

Black
White
Blue
Gold
Saddle

Johan's 1970 Olds 442 kit, when built box stock, gives a very nice model.

With a few extra parts and decals, your model can take on a new personality.

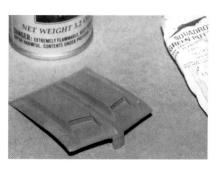

The mail-order hood in primer shows any and all imperfections. This hood is one of MPB Detail Products' first efforts, molded in a red dental resin.

MPB Detail Products' second effort was this two-piece W-30 hood. Note how much lower the scoops are compared to the original.

Holes for hood pins were already recessed in the hood.

All American Models has a one-piece W-30 hood in a more common resin. The hood also has the pins already molded in.

tion about someone who was casting W-30 hoods. I ordered the hood, not knowing what to expect. It arrived with a letter stating that the hood would probably be a rough fit. I was a bit apprehensive, but attempted to fit the hood and was pleasantly surprised to find that it fit perfectly. The hood surface did need some prep with putty and sanding to smooth it out. Then I primed it and put it aside to be painted later with the body. The twin scoops were a bit tall, but did not detract too much from the model's appearance. This hood was a first attempt for MPB Detail Products, cast from a red dental material that was extremely brittle. Later attempts from MPB Detail Products would yield the trademark two-piece vacu-formed hood in the correct configuration and proportions. All American Models also produces a one-piece W-30 hood in resin that can be purchased separately, which was first made for the 1970 442 convertible resin body.

19

The engine was built box stock, painted with Testor's Model Master Olds engine blue and further detailed with paint. I used a chromed dual-snorkel air cleaner from the scrap box in place of the kit air cleaner. I detailed the rest of the engine compartment with paint and painted the fender wells in the engine compartment red to match information I found in car magazines.

The chassis was a one-piece molded unit and lent itself to detailing with silver and steel paint. Since I built this model, ERTL has released a 1969 442 kit with a highly detailed chassis. In my opinion, this kit would be the building option of choice if you are looking for a higher level of detail for your 1970 442.

The kit tires were less than adequate, so I mated AMT/ERTL L60 x 15, Goodyear Polyglas GTs to the kit wheels. I detailed the wheels by painting the lug nut wells flat black, then accented the center crest with Testor's Model Master marker light red. I located wheel backs and metal

The Olds dash and interior has lots of woodgrain trim. A color magazine shot or a dealer brochure will help greatly when detailing.

axles in the parts box—the wheel backs in the kit tended to fall through the tire.

The interior was also molded as one unit except for the dash. I painted the dash flat black and detailed it as shown in the dealer literature—woodgrain detail was abundant in an Olds.

I sanded the body to remove mold lines and primed it. Then I spray-painted it with Testor's Model Master classic black, to simulate the Olds Ebony Black. Fred Cady supplies a very nice decal sheet with the W-30 stripes in both black and white—I chose the white stripes for my project. I detailed the chrome moldings with Bare Metal foil and chrome silver paint. After detailing it, I sprayed the entire body with

The dual snorkel air cleaner was not stock but looked better than the single snorkel unit supplied in the Johan kit. Since this was a low-tech conversion, I did not add any ignition wiring. All detailing was picked out with paint.

The mirrors were from a scrap box Mustang. Note the "W-30" under the 442 emblem—it adds a little extra appeal and detail to the model.

Testor's Glosskote. Then I painted the hood, applied the stripes, and glossed it. I also removed the 442 center crest from the Johan hood and glued it to the W-30 hood between the front grilles. The Fred Cady sheet provides rear stripes, but this was not a correct option for this model.

Photos and dealer brochures, as well as magazines, helped me place the decals. I painted mirrors from a scrap box Monogram Mustang Boss 429 to match the body color and epoxied them in place. I put the body, interior, glass, and chassis together, then located the front and rear bumpers and attached them with glue. I detailed the front grille with flat black paint and the turn signal lenses with Testor's Model Master turn signal amber.

This project was quick and very easy to build. It was designed as an exercise in low-tech model building, keeping the aftermarket parts to a minimum, yet yielding a nice finished product. As you can see, the results were well worth the effort.

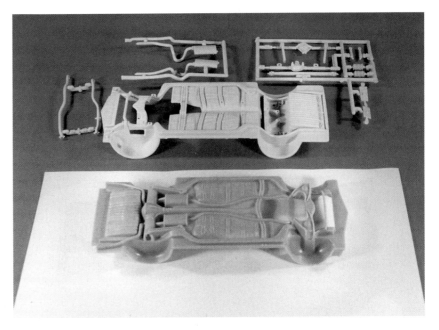

The Johan's kit chassis was a molded one-piece unit, whereas an ERTL 1969 442 kit's chassis is a multipieced unit that would make a nicer finished product.

The ERTL 1969 442, with some work, could also be used for engine parts, chassis detail, and interior in this conversion.

6
KILLER BEE

BUILDING A 1970 DODGE SUPER BEE

Have you ever wanted a model of a particular car so badly that you wound up sinking more money into it than you really wanted to? Well, here's my story. . . .

The summer of 1970 was a great time to be driving, because all around me was muscle. The newspapers and magazines were full of ads promoting raw street power. One ad in particular caught my eye then, and to this day it still puts a smile on my face. The ad showed a 1970 Dodge Coronet Super Bee leaving the "tree." The car had no emblems or stripes, but the radical new design made me take immediate notice. Most people thought that the 1970 Coronet was sinfully ugly—as one of my friends once

put it, "Kinda looks like a really bad blind date!" Frankly, GM's offerings received some criticism at that time, too.

The year 1970 was the last time the Dodge Super Bee was offered in the Coronet model line. It was available as a coupe or a hardtop, and the convertible was only available in the R/T version. A standard bumblebee wraparound stripe, which incorporated the crest, graced the rear of the body. A dramatic "C" stripe on the body sides was optional. Another stripe option, not listed but seen, was the stripe delete package; it gave the circular "Super Bee" crest on the rear quarter panel without a stripe. A 383-cubic-inch engine mated to a three-speed manual transmis-

sion was standard. Optional engines were the 440 six-pack and the 426 Hemi. Transmission options, in addition to the three speed, were a four-speed manual and an automatic. The standard hood was a power bulge with two razor-edge, nonfunctional scoops. If you ordered the Ramcharger option, the hood came with two separate scoops and a hood underside arrangement that allowed fresh air to enter the carburetor. The Ramcharger option was standard with the Hemi power plant. Wheel options included standard wheel covers, 14″ deep-dish steel wheels, wire wheel covers, Rallye Road wheels, 14″ or 15″ wheels, or chrome-styled road wheels (five spoke). Tire choices included

A "restified" 440 six-pack engine with aftermarket goodies. Note the lack of heater hoses—a street-vs.-race option.

white sidewall F70 x 14, F70 x 14 raised white letter, or F60 x 15 raised white letter.

Several years ago I wanted to build a 1970 Dodge Coronet Super Bee model, but the cost of a mint-condition unbuilt kit made this unattainable—this kit was rare! I eventually found a built car in rough shape, but the car had potential and I felt good that I didn't have to pay a mint for it. No sooner had I bought the car when a rumor surfaced that a resin body would be available. The project sat for a few years while I waited for the resin release. When the resin finally became available, I was a bit disappointed in that it was not the best casting I have ever seen. I tried to return the kit because of the flaws, but the caster was quick to point out that he was the only one casting a 1970 Coronet and that I should be happy with what I had. Both kits sat for several years while I decided what to do. The resin body needed quite a bit of cleaning up and body work to remove bumps, pinholes, and surface cracks. The original built model was missing the

stock interior, and it too needed body work. The tab was starting to add up. I now had a built-up original kit and a resin body, which cost me $57.00 total.

I finally decided to restore the original body, since it appeared to be the easier of the two to work with. The original body was hand-painted with gold—I should say, heavily painted with gold. I soaked the body in a solution of Pine-Sol for about 48 hours, and the paint washed away in a warm water rinse. This revealed many problems and quite a bit of glue damage. The kit chrome was poor, to say the least, but it was all there and the pieces were in good shape. I stripped the chrome using non-diluted Mr. Clean. This completely removes the chrome in a short amount of time, usually in about an hour, and is safe to use. I used warm water and a brush to removed embedded, stubborn chrome, then rinsed the parts clean. Then I packed up the parts and sent them to Chrome Tech for replating.

I spent the time without chrome working with the body.

My personal arsenal of polishes and wax

Side scoops had once been glued to the rear quarter panels, which left U-shaped glue pit marks in the plastic. I sanded the pits as smooth as I could to remove high spots, then filled in the low spots with Evercoat polyester glazing compound. This two-part putty is a pleasure to work with. It dries quickly, sands easily, and can be worked on in about 45 minutes. I applied additional coats as needed and wet-sanded it smooth. Then I sprayed Tempo sandable primer on the body.

After it was dry, I inspected the entire body, looking for additional problems. It's amazing how only one coat of primer revealed the additional work I needed to do! I removed mold lines, filled sink marks, and wet-sanded the body to almost-bare plastic. I applied another coat of sandable primer to fill previous sand marks and other imperfections. Since the body had no molded scripts, the painting process went very well. The third

coat of primer was a nonsandable primer. This lighter coat covered the bare plastic without obliterating details such as door locks or moldings.

After a light sanding and wash, I sprayed the body with five light coats of acrylic enamel in Plum Crazy. I wet-sanded each coat with 6000 grit sanding cloth, then washed and dried the body. Be careful when using the 6000 grit cloth—it tends to cut the paint right down to the primer at the high spots. With initial coats of paint this would not be a problem, but it could be with the final few coats. Next I rubbed out the paint with Mequiar's no. 5 and then no. 7 glaze, cleaned the body again, repainted with another coat, and sanded with 8000 grit polishing cloth. I repeated this process for all five coats of paint. Mequiar's no. 5 and no. 7 glazes are great to use; you can use them to rub out paint imperfections, and the polished surfaces can be repainted. If you

can't find Mequiar's products, you can substitute Bare Metal plastic polish—it too is paintable.

I applied a final "kiss-coat" of Plum Crazy and gently rubbed it to a high gloss. I applied Bare Metal foil to the moldings and placed a white Bumblebee stripe from Monogram's 1969 Super Bee kit around the rear of the car. I set the body aside to be waxed after final assembly. For waxing, I used the Micro Gloss Polish found in my polishing kit followed by Mequiar's no. 26 yellow wax.

The interior was very rough and the stock seats were missing. Johan's 1969 Roadrunner kit had incorrect 1970-style high-back bucket seats, and I just happened to have a parts kit with an extra set of seats. The seats did not match the interior pattern, but I was not too concerned. The kit interior appeared to be from a Charger and did not match the interior pictures I had from a real 1970 Coronet, anyway. One problem I encountered was that the seats were too low when set into the interior bucket—the headrest barely cleared the top of the door panel. I used a Plastruct I beam to achieve the correct height. This created another problem: The seat surface was now too high relative to the steering wheel, and needed to be angled upward to clear the raised seat. When I test-assembled the interior pieces, the completed interior did not look odd or out of place. Seats from MPC's 1971 Roadrunner could also be used.

Instrument panel detailing involved paint detailing the instrument faces and switches. I applied Bare Metal foil to the door panels and painted in "wood" between the foil. Since the interior was not accurate, it didn't matter if the wood graining was correct or not—I liked it, and that's what mattered. I

Goodyear F60-15s and Rallye wheels look much more at home than ERTL's standard issue L60-15s. The F60s are an easy conversion.

The original MPC 1970 Dodge Coronet Super Bee kit—very rare and expensive!

placed a vintage copy of *Super Stock* magazine on the front seat. The original automatic shifter was broken in three places and could not be repaired. I removed the shift knob from the original and drilled a hole into its base. I bent a straight pin, the same diameter as the drilled hole, to match the original shape and then epoxied it into the drilled hole. This delicate procedure took quite a bit of patience. I

set aside the completed interior until later.

Excellent sources for parts included the 1971 Roadrunner kit no. 6282 and the 1969 Dodge Daytona kit no. 6278, both from MPC. I used seats, six-pack engine parts, and the Rallye wheels from the Roadrunner kit. The chassis and exhaust came from the 1969 Daytona kit. I considered using the chassis from the 1968 Roadrunner for greater

detail, but I wanted this restoration to be as close to original as possible. The original engine was one horrific glue-blob mess and proved to be totally useless. I found a replacement block, originally from an MPC 1967 Charger kit, in a parts box. I easily adapted the six-pack parts to the Hemi block. If you cannot locate an automatic block, the model can be converted into a manual transmission car. A four-speed engine and transmission are available in the 1971 Roadrunner kit. I wired the engine and detailed the hose. I used yellow Detail Master wire to depict aftermarket Accel ignition wire. I took exhaust headers from the 1971 Roadrunner kit, painting them flat black to resemble Cassler headers, and tied them into the stock exhaust system.

The chassis from the 1969 Daytona had a separate exhaust system with mufflers, resonators, and exhaust tips. I painted the chassis with polished steel and buffed it. I painted the rest of the drivetrain gloss black and painted the chassis flat black with gloss frame rails.

I used L60-15 Goodyear tires because they filled the wheel well completely. In my opinion, L60 tire labels don't look right on the front of a car. I carefully cut away the horizontal part of the L and then hand-painted two horizontal lines to make an F—F60-15s are correct for this car. Since the tires were 15 inchers, I had to go with the Rallye wheel. I detailed the wheels with matte aluminum on the wheel surface itself, leaving a chrome trim ring. I painted the center caps gunmetal. For valve stems, I used a short piece of MSC black ignition wire. This wheel and tire combination really sets off the car. If you prefer a street machine look, Cragar mags or

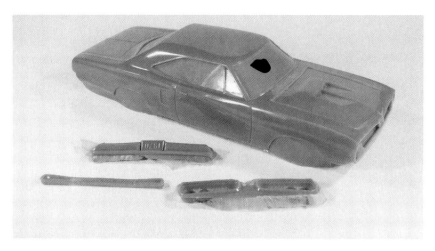

The resin body kit

The various parts kits used in this resto project: 1971 Roadrunner, 1969 Dodge Daytona, and 1969 GTX Pro Streeter

Keystone Klassics are the way to go. Remember to detail the center cap.

Next, I put together the subassemblies. I polished the glass to near-new appearance and epoxied the glass into the body. I painted the inside of the body flat black and glued in the completed interior. I laid the chassis with the engine into the body, but initially it looked saggy. I used Plastruct tubing as spacers between the chassis and the body in the trunk area. The body and chassis had four flat spots in this area, so the spacers fit perfectly.

The chrome finally arrived, and it looked great. I detailed the front grille with flat black in the grille area and painted matte aluminum on the surrounding trim. The taillights were badly broken, heavily glued, and unusable. I trimmed clear sheet plastic to the approximate shape of the taillight lens, backed it with Bare Metal foil, and painted with Tamiya clear red. Then I glued the lights to the chrome taillight panel and glued

the completed panel to the body.

Finishing touches included an Arkansas "BEE STING" rear plate and a "DODGE" front plate. These items are available from Scale Vanities. I took a door rearview mirror from ERTL's 1969 GTX Pro Streeter kit no. 6804. I also used an S&S Specialties (now named Detail Resources) radio antenna, but be aware that this item is no longer available from them.

Once the body was in color, I learned of ERTL's possible reissue of the 1970 Coronet. Oh well, stung again! A reissue would definitely be the way to go with this project, but I was impatient. Restoring a built kit is the next-best choice, depending on the kit's condition and completeness. Prices of restorables are beginning to climb, and price should be a major deciding factor when comparing a resto with a resin. Sometimes it's a tough choice. Don't buy a restorable kit if irreplaceable parts are missing or if there is major body damage. Pass on it, or the project will

become a bottomless money pit. You can remove a bad roof and turn the car into a convertible, but this takes some advanced skills—without these skills, the project could become very expensive and frustrating. In this instance, a resin body may be the way to go. You need some special skills to work with resins, but the car will not need to be hacked apart to make an acceptable model.

As my story ends, the final tab for my project car was $85.00. This included parts kits, a resin body that I'll never use, and the built Coronet.

One final piece of advice: Be honest with yourself and your skill level. Build for yourself, and try to improve with each new model. Don't be afraid to try new techniques or products, but don't try them all on one project—if you do, you'll probably give up modeling for good. Heed my advice, and you won't get stung on your next project!

7
CHEAP SIX-PACK
BUILDING A 1969 PLYMOUTH ROADRUNNER 440 6-BBL

In the spring of 1969 Plymouth introduced a new version of the Roadrunner simply called the 440 6-bbl. The engine was a 390 hp, specially modified 440 cubic inch with three two-barrel carbs on an aluminum Edelbrock manifold. In 1969 NHRA had factored the engine at 410 hp. The special engine modifications included stiffer Hemi valve springs, a low taper camshaft with special lifters, chromed valve stems, Moly filled top piston rings, a dual point distributor, Hemi-type connecting rods, and a roller timing chain with a three-bolt sprocket. These modifications allowed the shift points to be around the 6500 mark. A four-speed transmission with Hurst shifter or Torqueflite automatic was standard. Other standard features included heavy-duty 11-inch drum brakes, Hemi-type rear springs, a heavy-duty cooling system, a 4.10:1 Sure-Grip rear differential, a 9 3/4″ ring and pinion Dana rear, and Goodyear G70 x 15 Red Streak tires mounted to 15 x 6 black steel wheels with chrome lug nuts. The car had a distinctive flat black fiberglass hood with a large scoop. On either side of the scoop was a decal boasting engine displacement. The hood was held down with four locking pins and needed two people to be handled—very impressive at the gas station when the attendant asked, "Can I check your oil?" The hood was engineered to boost horsepower by 20 at 100 miles per hour. The car was avail-

able in five Chrysler colors: Vitamin C Orange, Performance Red, Bahama Yellow, Rallye Green, and white. If you picked up any automotive magazine of that era, you would find that the 440 was a very powerful power plant. It rivaled the Hemi in power, yet was much easier to maintain.

In 1973 I didn't think much of my friend's car until I rode in it. Today I can dream of those days and recall them in plastic.

To build a 1969 Roadrunner 440 6-bbl replica you will need the following: Johan's 1969 Roadrunner kit no. 2200, MPC's 1971 Roadrunner kit no. 6282, and Monogram's 1969 Superbee kit no. 2215. The basic conversion can be made from these three kits. Since I completed my conversion, Scale Speed Shop released a complete conversion kit in resin. Unfortunately, availability of this fine conversion kit may be limited. For my conversion, I chose to add extra detail and used parts from various parts kits as I will describe. From the Monogram kit, I used the

hood scoop, driver's door mirror, and air cleaner with the hood seal. You will also need a bench seat, which can be found in Revell's 1954 Chevy Panel Delivery kit no. 7139.

I removed the twin scoops from the Johan kit hood. First I used a Dremel tool to remove the bulk of the material, then I sanded the entire area as flat as I could. Some reissued versions of the 1969 Roadrunner may have a hood with the area under the scoops recessed. This won't work, because if you remove the scoops, you could go right through the hood. The most current reissues have a suitable hood. I used spot putty to help smooth out the area even further. I modified the hood scoop from the Monogram kit by removing the mounting lip on the bottom and sanding the top ridge flat. Then I glued the scoop to the Roadrunner hood and blended with some spot putty. I removed the Roadrunner name plate from the front edge of the hood. The real hood has a raised portion just in front of the scoop opening, but it was raised just

27

slightly so I omitted it from my model. The hood from Scale Speed Shop accurately depicts the real hood. If you desire a functional hood scoop, this is the time to open the underside of the hood.

After I completed all of the putty and sanding work, I sprayed the hood with primer and overcoated it with flat black. I added a 440 6-BBL decal from Fred Cady's decal sheet no. 282 to each side of the hood scoop. Then I overcoated the hood with Testor's Dullcote to seal the decals, as they tended not to stick to the flat black hood surface. I added hood pins from an old Chevette or Camaro parts kit (1974 to 1976 MPC vintage)—they seemed to be the best suited for the project at that time. Another option is to use photoetched hood pins from Detail Master. Remember that four hood pins are needed, one at each corner of the hood. I put the hood aside until later.

The chassis was a dull, one-piece unit common to most Johan kits of that vintage. A better option is the chassis from one of the more recent AMT/ERTL kits, specifically from the 1969 GTX convertible kit no. 6429, the 1969 GTX Hardtop kit no. 6111, or the 1968 Roadrunner kit no. 6515. I placed the axle locators in the Johan chassis and painted it flat black, painting the frame rails gloss black. Then I painted the exhaust pieces with Monogram's Metalcote polished steel and buffed them when dry. Other molded detail was lacking and the model would benefit from chassis detailing, but I chose not to detail it any further.

I took the engine from the MPC 1971 Roadrunner kit no. 6282 and modified it slightly to fit the Johan chassis. I added a piece of plastic rod to the rear of

the transmission to extend the tail shaft, and I made new engine mounts from scrap plastic. I dechromed the chrome valve covers, oil pan, and fan by letting them soak in Mr. Clean for a few hours. I painted the assembled engine block with Testor's Chevy engine orange (can you hear the Mopar purists?) just to make it a shade different from the orange body. At this time I also removed the power steering pump and belt. I used the air cleaner from the Monogram kit—which is mixing scales, but if you have ever seen a real 440 6-bbl air cleaner, it's massive. I achieved the right look here by mixing scales. For added detail, I placed drain hoses at the front of the lower air cleaner pan. Some literature shows these hoses at opposite corners, yet some shows them as I placed them. I wired the engine and further detailed it with heater and radiator hoses, then glued the entire assembly in place. I simulated hose clamps using $1/64''$ chrome striping tape. I could not use the front axle unless I drilled through the engine block, so I used an alternate method to mount the tires.

I took tires from the scrap box, which originally came from a MPC Corvette or Impala kit and depicted Goodyear G70 x 15s. These tires are my personal favorite because of the stock, wide-tread look. I "redlined" them as described in Chapter 9. These particular tires were easy to detail since I only had to adjust the bow compass onto the raised sidewall outline—I couldn't go wrong! Of course, I sanded the tire tread. The stock kit wheels were a bit too deep, but could be used. I used wheels from a friend's parts box, which originally came from an old 1966 Charger kit. The wheels had that Chrysler look but lacked front

The engine shows the results of using various scales to achieve the desired effect.

bearing dust caps, which I scratchbuilt from oil breather caps I found in the 1969 Roadrunner kit. Wheels found in Johan's 1964 Dodge kit no. 2864 can also be used. They would need to be dechromed and are actually slightly smaller in diameter, which may require that they be epoxied to the tire. Resin copies of the standard Chrysler steel wheels can be obtained from The Good Stuff. My wheels were painted black and the lug nuts detailed with chrome silver. I detailed the front wheel bearing dust caps with a bit of brass paint. I oversprayed the completed wheels with Testor's semi-gloss clear, epoxied them to the tires and wheel backs, and set them aside for final assembly.

The interior needed a taxi-cab look and since I wasn't about to recreate the stock seat pattern, I chose to do a generic replica with a spartan look. I used the bench seat from the 1954 Chevy, removing the bottom trim piece of the seat with a X-acto blade. This gave the seat more of an angle when I placed it flat. I removed the upholstery pattern and added a seat back with sheet plastic. I also removed the seat pattern on the kit's back seat, using a Dremel tool. After I sanded them smooth, I masked off the tops of both seats along with the front of the seat bottoms.

I made the taxicab bench seat I wanted using a bench seat from a 1954 Chevy panel truck and a paint technique described in the text. The head rests were modified Camaro units mounted with straight pins—and by the way, they are functional.

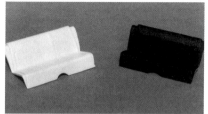

I modified the rear seat in the same way.

The stock kit interior compared to the taxi interior

Then, using black wrinkle paint, I sprayed the exposed areas and put the parts under a lamp to let the paint wrinkle. Be careful not to set the bulb of the lamp too close to the plastic, or it will melt. Don't worry if the paint goes on too thick—the thicker the better, because you will get more texture. When the paint was semidry, I added a seam between the textured and smooth area with $1/64''$ striping tape. Then I sprayed the entire seat with flat black.

You can make working headrests by filing down headrests from MPC's 1969 Camaro about a third and cutting straight pins to use as mounting posts. These will mount to the top of the front seats. If the pins are long enough, the headrests will actually adjust to height. I oversprayed the interior shell, seats, and detailed dash with Testor's semigloss and assembled them when they were dry.

I used a shifter from Monogram's 1970 Chevelle since it resembled a Hurst unit, removing the shifter ball (which was not perfectly round) and replacing it with a ball from a straight pin. For extra realism, I used the steering wheel from Monogram's 1970 GTX kit no. 2730. I paint detailed the horn rim with chrome silver, painted the center of the wheel horn button white, and added a Roadrunner head decal to the recessed horn button. This decal came from the MPC Roadrunner kit no. 6282 decal sheet.

When first attempting to build the coupe I tried to fashion the window pillars from Evergreen plastic, but soon found them included in the kit—it pays to read the instruction sheet. I filled in the sink marks on the body, sanded the area smooth, and painted the entire body flat white. If you use an antenna, drill the hole at this time on the top of the passenger-side fender. I sprayed the body, fire wall, radiator support, and fender wells with Testor's orange, right from the can. I detailed the moldings with Bare Metal foil and picked up other details with silver paint. I painted the window pillars to match the body color and painted the inside surfaces silver. I used Bare Metal foil to detail all of the Roadrunner script. I flowed Tamiya smoke onto the lettering and immediately buffed the high spots with a paper towel to give the lettering depth and definition. I detailed the bird emblem by painting the feathers purple, the beak yellow, and the legs red. When it was dry, I overcoated the entire body with Testor's Glosscote. Then I epoxied in the glass, completed interior, and chassis.

I detailed the grille with thinned flat black paint, which flowed into all the grille recesses and around the headlights. I painted the headlight bezels with flat aluminum to simulate argent. The lenses were a poor fit and needed several trial fits and some work before they fit well. Once I achieved the proper fit, I glued in the lenses with white glue. I glued the rear lights into the bezels, then placed them into the recesses in the rear panel. Remember to paint the area around the red lens with flat aluminum. This was common to the cheaper models, as flat black was used on the GTX models.

The front bumper mounts were very fragile and should be handled carefully. In my construction I was not so careful, and I lost both mounts. I mounted the front bumper by gluing it to the inner lip on the body. This actually brought the bumper up to an acceptable height. The rear bumper mounting holes were too low, so I elongated them so that the bumper could be moved upward to a

The kit hood needed to have the Hemi scoops removed. Be sure to use a later reissued kit, because earlier kits do not have enough plastic beneath the scoops and will sand through.

The scoop from Monogram's kit needed to have the ridge removed.

Comparing before (right) and after (left)—with plenty of spot putty, sanding, decals, and hood pins you can change the appearance completely.

Red line tire techniques add a special touch to your tire choice.

suitable location. If you do not do this, you will have an obvious gap between the bumper and the body—and nothing looks worse than a sagging bumper. I detailed the front turn signal indicators with Tamiya clear yellow and the rear indicators with Tamiya clear red. I painted the front bumper vent slats flat black. I glued the tires and wheels into the stock mounting holes, using a metal axle for the rear and a cut-down axle for the front.

The engine compartment had two plastic mounts molded to the underside to accommodate the hood lying in place, which needed no further modification. Other details included a battery with cables, washer bottle, and air cleaner decals. There was no documentation of any engine displacement decals for the air cleaner, only instructional decals. I made these decals by cutting a red "NO STEP" airplane decal in two and placing it in the appropriate places on top of the air cleaner. The decal appears to have writing on it, but it is so tiny that it cannot be read. The final assembly step was to epoxy an antenna into the predrilled

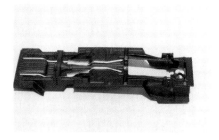

The kit chassis lacks detail, but with some Monogram Metalcote paint and patience it can look better.

hole on the fender and add "RUNNER" license plates to the car. I used scale rubber from D&J Enterprises to make the rubber floor mats, making a pattern by tracing the floor outline onto tissue paper. From this a template was made and fitted. Once the fit was obtained, I traced the outline onto the scale rubber and cut it. I added texture to the rubber by clamping the piece of rubber in a vise, allowing the pattern of the vise jaws to imprint the rubber.

I epoxied an authentic, cheap rearview mirror to the driver's door. This mirror came from the Monogram 1969 Superbee kit no. 2215.

I tied the stock MPC Roadrunner exhaust manifolds into

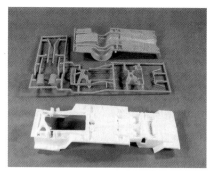

Chassis comparison between the Johan unit and the highly detailed AMT/ERTL unit

the chassis exhaust pipes using Auto World bendable rod, which is no longer available. Then I painted the pipes with Monogram Metalcote polished steel and buffed them. I made exhaust tips by cutting down 1970 GTX resonators and mating them to 1970 Chevelle exhaust tips. When properly trimmed, only $1/8''$ to $1/4''$ should show below the rear bumper.

The Johan kit alone is rather mundane in stock form, but with some imagination it can be enhanced and will really add something to your display shelf. I've owned the model for quite some time now—maybe I should consider Cragars, like Pete did!

8
SILENT PARTNER

BUILDING MONOGRAM'S 1971 'CUDA STREET MACHINE OR HEMICUDA INTO A 440 SIX-PACK VERSION

When people talk about a 1971 'Cuda, a Hemicuda instantly comes to mind. But the Hemi was not the only version made that year. The 440 six-pack version ran a close second in performance. The Hemi would certainly plant your molars in the back of your mouth, but it was a difficult engine to maintain and tune. The Hemi cars were owned by what appeared to be an elite group, as there just were not enough of these cars to go around—only 108 Hemicudas were produced in 1971. The 440 six-pack was no slouch when it came to performance; it even gave the Hemi cars a run for their money. A total of 237 440 six-pack 'Cudas were built. Of these, 108 were four-speed cars and 129 were automatics.

In 1972 a car dealer in our city sold "cream puffs"—pre-owned, high-performance cars. One morning I took a ride out to this dealership to see what he had in my price range. I spotted a beautiful red 1971 'Cuda with a white interior. The twin hood scoops boasted of a 440 six-pack. The salesman gave me the keys and said, "Give her a run on the stretch in the back!" The car almost didn't start because of a bad battery, but it eventually did. The pistol-grip shifter felt great, and the shifter slid into gear easily. After a sufficient warm-up period, I drove the car slowly to the stretch and thought that it just ran just okay—nothing to get

excited about. I then floored the gas pedal and felt my internal organs move toward the seat back as the other two carbs joined in. A quick jerk of the shifter, into second gear, threw me deeper into the seat—I was getting one wild test drive. I only had enough road left for one more gear, so I went for it. As the clutch disc made contact with the flywheel, the tires let out a healthy chirp. Sitting here now writing this, I'm getting goosebumps. When I returned the car to the spot where I found it, the salesman was standing there with the papers I needed to sign for ownership. I never bought that car, primarily because I took my dad for a ride in it and he smiled and said, "The insurance man isn't going to like this at all!" How right he was—I was destined to be caught in the insurance crunch of the 1970s.

The 'Cuda's basic body style was a carryover from 1970 with a

few cosmetic changes. The front end had four headlights instead of two, and the front fenders had simulated louvers above the wheel wells. There was also a slight change in the rear taillight. The front grille area was painted a bright silver, but if you ordered an elastomeric front bumper the grille area came painted body color. If you go to car shows you may spot a car with an elastomeric bumper and the grille area still painted bright silver. This may be an owner add-on, since I could not find any documentation of such a combination. Engine choices for 1971 included a standard 300 hp 383 four-barrel, an optional 275 hp 340 four-barrel, an optional 385 hp 440 six-barrel, and the infamous 425 hp eight-barrel 426 Hemi. The 440 four-barrel was dropped in 1971. Of the 440 six-barrel production, 237 were hardtops and 17 were convertibles. Billboard rear fender engine

Exterior Colors and Codes

Winchester Gray Metallic	GA4
Glacial Blue Metallic	GB2
True Blue Metallic	GB5
Evening Blue Metallic	GB7
Amber Sherwood Metallic	GF3
Sherwood Green Metallic	GF7
Autumn Bronze Metallic	GK6
Tunisian Tan Metallic	GT2
Sno White	GW3
Formal Black	TX9
Gold Leaf Metallic	GY8
Tawny Gold Metallic	GY9
In Violet	FC7
Sassy Grass Green	FV6
Bahama Yellow	EG5
Tor-Red	EV2
Curious Yellow	GY3
Lemon Twist	FY1

Interior Colors

Black
Blue
Green
Tan
White/Black
Gold
Black/Orange

Vinyl Roof Colors

Black
White

Convertible Top Colors

Black
White

The 440 engine from Monogram's 1970 GTX 2 'n 1 kit drops right in with only minor modifications.

Monogram's 1971 'Cuda Street Machine kit and 1970 GTX kit are the basis for a 1971 440 six-pack 'Cuda.

displacement decals were standard but could be deleted.

I felt it would be appropriate to capture the memory of that morning in 1972 with a model. I really had not planned to write about this conversion, but it came out well and I tried a few new things, so I felt it should be shared.

When I purchased the Monogram 1971 'Cuda Street Machine kit no. 2701 at the local hobby shop, the kid behind the counter smugly said, "Oh, wow!" I was determined not to let him intimidate me—I held my head high, looked him in the eye, and said, "No, I don't need a bag." The box art may scare some people off, but it really is a nice kit to build. There are still plenty of these kits around, even though Monogram dropped it from the 1988 catalog. Monogram still has the 1971 Hemicuda available, and combined with a resin twin scoop hood from Muscle in Miniature, the trappings for this project are still available. You will also need to purchase Monogram's 1970 GTX kit no. 2730, primarily for the 440 six-pack engine. If you wish to build an automatic version, you will also need Monogram's 1971 Satellite kit no. 2213, which has a 440 four-barrel engine mated to an automatic transmission.

If you build a four-speed version, as I did, all you need to do is build the GTX engine as it comes from the box. The stock exhaust manifolds work without any chassis modification. You need to notch out the trans mount on the chassis so that the trans mount on the transmission will drop lower into the chassis.

You may choose instead to remove some material from the trans mount. Either method will lower the transmission sufficiently. I ground off the motor mounts approximately 1/8″ to make it sit lower in the chassis. I also found it necessary to sand down the carbs a bit so that the air cleaner would fit under the hood. I painted the engine block with Testor's Chrysler engine red enamel and the transmission with Monogram's Metalcote polished steel. The Monogram paint is great to work with—it dries flat, and after about 30 minutes you buff the painted part with a cloth. After buffing it, you would swear that the part is really metal. Note that this paint is no longer available; a reasonable substitute is Testor's Metallizer paint. I left the air cleaner and the valve covers chromed. I painted the air cleaner element flat white and the bottom pan semigloss black—I always liked the Direct Connection aftermarket parts. I wired the block with ignition wires and added a Fred Cady engine displacement decal to the top of the detailed air cleaner. Then I put the completed engine aside for a while. If you choose to build the automatic car, use the 440 engine block and transmission from the Satellite kit and add the six-pack intake.

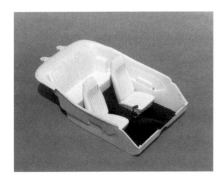

A white interior can really make a dark body color stand out. The 'Cuda kit interior is basic, and the lack of a console makes the pistol-grip shifter stand out.

A new and different experience: painting Monogram's Metalcote polished steel on a molded exhaust system

Metalcoat dries flat but, when buffed, really makes the part stand out. The transmission can also benefit from an application. Simple paint and patience can bring a chassis alive.

I painted the chassis flat black and accented the frame rails with gloss black, then detailed the cables and fuel lines with silver paint. I raised the rear using the 'Cuda kit's suspension risers so that I could fit a larger rear tire. In the past I have received several comments about using Otaki tires on my models, but not everyone has access to them. With this conversion I used Monogram's big and little Goodyear GT Radials; I found the complete front and rear set in Monogram's Heavy Chevy Chevelle 3 'n 1 kit no. 2715. I chose the Magnum 500 mag from the GTX kit and carefully detailed both the tires and the wheels. The 'Cuda kit has one drawback: The chassis has a molded-on exhaust, which I personally do not care for. But here the Monogram Metalcote paint worked like a charm. I carefully painted the exhaust pipes and mufflers with the Metalcote polished steel and, when dry, buffed it to a gloss. I can not describe in words the improvement it made to the chassis—I hope the photos give you a better idea of what to expect.

The interior as it comes from the box is rather plain. There is no console (a resin console is available from Muscle in Miniature, if you desire one), but its absence really makes the pistol-grip shifter stand out. I painted the interior seats and door panels white with contrasting black carpeting, steering wheel center, and dash. I added woodgrain to the area surrounding the instruments and around the pistol-grip shifter. I detailed the instrument faces with silver paint, using a dry-brushing technique: Dip the tip of a very fine brush in the paint and paint the excess onto a 3 x 5 card, then run the nearly dry brush over the numerals. This way you won't put a big paint blob on the gauge face. Once the paint dried, I placed a drop of Micro Kristal-Kleer, which is available in hobby shops, into each gauge. It looks like glorified white glue, but dries clear and gives the gauges the appearance of being under glass. I painted the rubber boot flat black to simulate black rubber. If you desire an automatic version, you can simply add the resin console mentioned earlier and remove the clutch pedal from the 'Cuda interior.

I sanded the body and primed it with Testor's light gull gray paint. This is a military flat, but it makes a great primer if you use a bright body color. Then I airbrushed the body using Chrysler engine red enamel —I liked it so much on the engine that I decided it would look great on the body. I masked the rear light panel, sprayed it flat black, and detailed it with Bare Metal foil. The front grille and front pan are one unit, so I masked the red and sprayed the top half bright silver, which I made by mixing Testor's Model Masters steel in a 2:1 mixture. I painted the accents with Testor's chrome silver and detailed the grille recesses with flat black. I also detailed the fender vents with the bright silver mixture, then outlined the vents outlined with Bare Metal.

One of my biggest problems recently has been with dust and airbrushing. It seems that no matter how careful I am, dust still finds its way onto a freshly painted surface. This was the case with the 'Cuda. When this happened in the past I would sand the entire body down and try a color coat again—but this became quite frustrating. Recently I acquired an LMG Enterprises Micro-Mesh polishing kit and figured I had nothing to lose in trying it, since I probably needed to repaint the body

Another first: using the Micro-Mesh polishing system from LMG. It includes various grades of very fine sandpaper, a foam sanding block, a flannel polishing cloth, and a bottle of polishing cream. You can get good results with only a little effort. Note the reflection on the door panel.

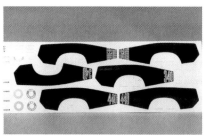

Excellent billboard decals are available from Fred Cady.

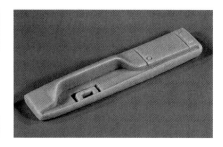

If you want a console for your four-speed car or if you plan to build an automatic version, Muscle in Miniature offers a resin console.

anyway. Was I ever surprised! I used the finest grit sanding cloth from the kit, and the dust particle was forever gone. I initially followed the sanding with the polishing creme, which also removed overspray that had dried on the surface. I polished half the hood and saw that it made an obvious improvement. Then I applied Bare Metal to the moldings. I tried to use the new Gunze Foil, but had some difficulty getting used to it. It is thinner than the Bare Metal and much softer, making the surface easier to mar. I will need to experiment and practice more before I feel comfortable using it.

I added two 440 six-pack decals from a Fred Cady decal sheet to the twin hood scoops. When I first started this project no one offered the Billboard engine displacement decal, so I took the decal delete option. Fred Cady now offers the Billboard decals in 340, 383, 440, and Hemi versions, in both black and white.

After the body was completely detailed, I sprayed it with Testor's Glosscote to add a little extra depth to the paint. Much to my horror, the paint started to bead. Rather than try to strip the paint, I decided to buy another

kit and start the body from square one. Instead of polishing the paint, I sanded out the dust particles, sprayed the Glosscote, and sanded the dry body with the 8000-grit sanding cloth. This removed any orange-peel look and left a smooth base for the polishing creme. After a good workout with a soft cloth, the paint came alive.

I detailed the engine compartment with paint and flexible radiator hoses. I detailed the ends of the upper hose with some $1/32''$ chrome stripping tape to simulate hose clamps. Then I epoxied the glass to the body. I recently discovered that, over time, styrene cement will distort the plastic—especially if you run a bead of glue along the clear connecting bars on the windshield and glue it to the roof interior.

Now the engine is ready to be glued to the chassis. Also, the exhaust manifolds need to be tied to the pipes. I have found that Plastruct or bendable rod from Auto World works well in this application. The driveshaft also needs to be shortened a small amount.

I epoxied the front grille/bumper assembly in place after

gluing in the chassis. I also glued the rear bumper and valance panel at this time. The final details were to paint the fog lamps, parking lights, and side marker lights with Tamiya's clear orange and clear red, and to epoxy the side mirrors to the doors. These can either be painted with a body color, as I did, or chrome. Then I added "Cuda" license plates from the kit and placed a radio antenna on top of the rear fender. I have seen pictures in which the antenna appears to be mounted on the front passenger side fender, but the car I drove had a dealer-installed radio and the antenna was mounted on the rear fender.

After the model had dried for several seeks, I waxed the entire car with The Treatment Car Wax. This removed all fingerprints and brought the finish to a deep luster—I almost sound like a commercial.

The 'Cuda was an easy conversion and it would have been more fun to do if I hadn't goofed with the body. This conversion basically consisted of just swapping parts. I'm sure that if you give it a try you'll see how well it can go.

9
MUSCLE CAR TIRES

Many of the new and old kit releases from the model manufacturers build into really nice models, but I always felt that something was lacking. One evening, at a model car meeting, one of the members gave a demonstration of how to "redline" the kit tires on Monogram's GTO. This small addition gave the model a highly desired period look.

In this chapter we'll discuss muscle car tires in detail and the technique involved in "lining" your own kit tires.

First, let's look at a tire comparison chart, paying attention to actual 1:1 tire dimensions and how they relate to various model

kit tires, which should give you an idea of how to size real tires. The scale tire comparison chart shows how model tires "size up."

Once you decide what size tire to use, you need to choose the type of tire sidewall. Redlines were used in the mid-1960s until 1969, when white-lettered tires began to dominate the option choice. "Goldline" tires were specialty tires that appeared on cars like Corvettes and the 1965 Z-16 Chevelle—a special car needed a special tire. Other cars may have also had these tires as well. Use your reference material or personal preference as a guide to help you decide what type of tire sidewall to make.

How to Redline Tires

Material used to detail tires includes a bow compass with pen adapter, tires of choice, and Monogram/Humbrol no. 153 flat red enamel paint. Other brands of flat red may be used as well. For whitelines use Testor's flat white or Tamiya flat white no. XF-2. For goldlines, Polly-S no. 400432 CP yellow may be used. For bluelines, use Testor's French blue. Be sure the wheels have a center hole at the same height as the tire sidewall.

1:1 Tire Size Chart

Series	Width	Height
E78 x 14	5.10˝	26.60˝
F78 x 14	5.25˝	27.06˝
G78 x 14	5.38˝	27.10˝
G78 x 15	5.63˝	27.68˝
H78 x 15	5.74˝	28.36˝
L78 x 15	5.88˝	29.30˝
D70 x 14	6.20˝	25.40˝
F70 x 14	6.00˝	26.00˝
G70 x 14	6.50˝	26.60˝
D60 x 14	7.00˝	24.70˝
G60 x 14	8.00˝	25.20˝
L60 x 14	9.50˝	27.50˝
H50 x 14	9.50˝	25.30˝
N50 x 14	11.00˝	26.90˝
F70 x 15	6.00˝	26.60˝
G70 x 15	6.50˝	27.50˝
C60 x 15	6.00˝	25.00˝
F60 x 15	8.80˝	25.90˝
G60 x 15	8.00˝	26.40˝
L60 x 15	9.50˝	27.40˝
H50 x 15	10.00˝	26.00˝
N50 x 15	11.00˝	27.50˝

On some models you may need to use a wheel back pushed in from the back to attain the proper center height.

Remove any flash from the sidewalls of the kit tires. Use the side of the tire without any raised lettering.

Tighten the pen thumbscrew to achieve a very small opening, about the same thickness as a 3 x 5 card.

Snap the wheel centers into the tire.

Place the compass point into the hole in the wheel center. Bring the pen onto the middle of the sidewall by adjusting the thumbscrew in the center of the compass. This brings the compass arms closer together.

When you are satisfied with the centering, stir the paint and, using a brush, apply a liberal amount of paint into the pen. Hold the point downward and allow the paint to flow toward the tip. You should have paint only on the inside of the paint tip.

Scale Tire Comparison Chart

Type of Model Kit Tire

	Scale width	Scale height	1:1 width	1:1 height
T/A Radial (R) Otaki	0.5″	1.13″	12″	27.12″
T/A Radial (F) Otaki	0.44″	1.0″	10.6″	24.00″
Goodyear Speedway Wide Tread F70 x 15 MPC	0.25″	1.06″	6.25″	26.50″
Goodyear Custom Wide Tread Polyglas MPC	0.31″	1.06″	7.75″	26.50″
Goodyear Rally GT (R) AMT	0.44″	1.06″	11.0″	26.50″
Goodyear Rally GT (F) AMT	0.38″	0.97″	9.50″	24.25″
Goodyear Polyglas GT F60 x 15 MPC	0.25″	1.00″	6.25″	25.00″
Goodyear Polyglas GT L60 x 15 ERTL	0.34″	1.03″	8.50″	25.75″
Goodyear Polyglas GT L60 x 15 AMT	0.38″	1.06″	9.50″	26.50″
Goodyear Rally GT L60 x 15 Monogram	0.44″	1.06″	10.60″	26.50″
Goodyear Rally GT F60 x 15 Monogram	0.31″	1.00″	7.44″	24.00″
Goodyear Radial GT Monogram (little)	0.38″	1.09″	9.12″	26.16″
Goodyear Radial GT Monogram (big)	0.38″	1.19″	9.12″	28.56″
Michelin TRX Monogram	0.28″	1.00″	6.72″	24.00″
Firestone Super Sports F70 x 15 ERTL	0.31″	1.00″	7.75″	25.00″

Place the compass point into the wheel center and touch the pen tip to the tire. Now in one smooth motion, mark the sidewall with paint. If the tip is set too wide, paint will flow onto the tire in a glob. To correct this, tighten the thumbscrew. If you goof, wipe off the error with a thinner-soaked rag and try again. Do all four tires at the same time, being sure to leave the wheel centers in until the paint dries.

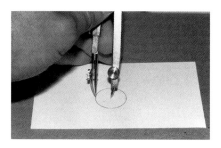

If you are too shaky or just need a bit more confidence, try working on a 3 x 5 card until you get the feel of the compass.

The finished tires in 1/24 and 1/25 scale next to a tire from Stevens International

10
WHEEL-DEEPENING TECHNIQUES

Over the years I have often been approached at shows and asked, "Where did you get those wheels?" I always enjoy the look on people's faces when I tell them that the wheels came directly from the kit! I quickly follow this statement with the disclaimer that the wheels were modified slightly from box stock configuration. The most radical difference in wheel look can be seen with the GTO wheels in Chapter 1. These wheels were box stock with the addition of deeper trim rings in the rear and a fuller looking trim ring in front. The difference from box stock was night and day, since the box stock wheels resembled only the center section of a GTO wheel and not a fully trim-ring-complemented wheel.

Sometimes my projects required a special look when it came to wheels. A custom or billet wheel may not have been needed, but a stock wheel of a slightly different, deeper dimension. At other times the wheel choice appropriate for a conversion did not properly fit the tire of choice. Here a deeper wheel may not have been appropriate, but a larger diameter trim ring would have worked better. A very simple solution to this problem involves swapping outer wheel rims of the appropriate size, matched with the wheel of choice. You can find wheel rims in many kits, sometimes in chrome and sometimes in just plain plastic.

Consider the possibilities. Deeper steel rims with a dog-dish hubcap could look great on just about any sleeper muscle car. The following pictures will guide you through the process of selecting and creating the wheels you need in the appropriate depth or diameter. In addition, aftermarket companies offer aluminum trim rings of various depths and diameters that can enhance any project.

Select your tire and wheel combination. Whether you want to achieve a change in diameter or change in depth, the technique will be the same. You may find the correct size wheel rim in the donor kit, but with a center that is undesirable.

Take the desired wheel center and sand the outer top rim down to bare plastic. This gives the new rim a place to grip when glued.

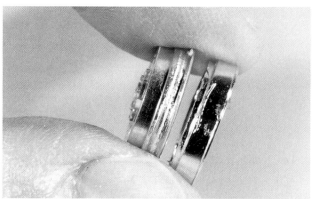

Test fit the donor rim with the desired tire. Using the donor rim, you can either sand the back of the rim until the center section drops out or, using a razor saw, you can cut out the center section by working around the donor rim.

The donor rim needs to be sanded flat so that it mates properly to the desired wheel center.

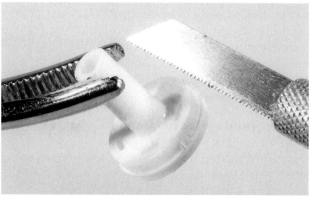

A coarse sandpaper such as a 320 grit, taped to a flat surface, will give you a flat mating surface. Be sure to go slowly with the sandpaper. Apply cement such as Plastruct Plastic Weld to the mating surfaces and allow the assemblies to dry before working with the wheels any further.

If the wheel backs have an extended axle shaft, be sure to trim this if needed to achieve proper ride track.

Aftermarket aluminum trim rings can save a lot of time, but should not be used in chrome wheel applications. After all, it is aluminum!

MAIL-ORDER MUSCLE

BUILDING A BALDWIN-MOTION 1970 CHEVELLE

I had filled out the order blank and checked it twice, but had only the $256.00 I had saved from cutting lawns. Not quite enough! My Chevelle was not to be.

While I was visiting my mom one weekend, she produced a box of stuff that she wanted me to go through before she tossed it. Upon close inspection, I realized she had stumbled upon a box from my old room that contained valuable car stuff dating back to 1970. Amidst the dealer brochures and speed catalogs was a neatly printed order blank for the 1970 Phase III Motion Chevelle. Had I ordered the car in 1970, it would have been the thirteenth Chevelle—only 12 such cars were ever produced.

I had ordered my phantom thirteenth car with the 500 hp, 454-cubic-inch Phase III engine, rock-crusher M-21 four-speed Muncie gear box, Lakewood scatter shield, and a Hurst super shifter with reverse lockout and line lock. This option list lent itself to a console delete, gauges under the dash and a Stahl mechanical tachometer on the steering column. The red exterior was accented with custom striping and a Green Meanie L-88-type fiberglass hood. The engine did all its exhaling through a pair of Hooker side mount exhausts, done up in Spartan flat black. The Goodyear Polyglas tires mounted on Cragar rims transferred the power to the pavement.

When I think about it now, this car was quite a handful for a

Monogram's Heavy Chevy Chevelle kit has odd box art but can build up into a nice-looking kit. I used it as the basis for my conversion. Revell's 1968 Corvette kit sacrificed a hood, and the versatile Rampage Camaro kit supplied many speed goodies.

kid of 16. Today, with this order blank in hand, I decided to build the phantom thirteenth Motion Chevelle in scale.

I started with Monogram's 1970 Chevelle kit no. 2715. The first order of business was to make that special Green Meanie L-88 hood. I used the extra, flat blower-type hood from the Chevelle kit and mated the scoop from the L-88 1968 Corvette, Revell kit no. 7159. I cut the scoop out of the Corvette hood, sanded it to match the contour of the Chevelle hood, and glued it to the Chevelle hood. I molded the scoop into the Chevelle hood using Evercoat filler. Be sure that the scoop is securely bonded to

the hood, or it may crack with normal handling.

Next, I decided to tackle the problem of the consoled interior. If you really want a console, just leave it in and save yourself a lot of conversion work. I chose to remove the console by trimming around its perimeter with the back of a no. 11 X-acto blade. Try to make many light passes around the console, remove a small bit of plastic with each pass, and eventually the console will pop right out. Cover the opening with masking tape, turn the interior over, and fill the hole with epoxy. The epoxy will flow into the hole and conform to the masking tape mold. Remove

The blower-type hood from the Chevelle kit works as a great base for the L-88 scoop from the Corvette hood. The L-88 scoop must be cut from the Corvette hood.

The marriage of plastic can be beautiful. Here is the completed hood.

The interior without a console shows the Detail Master pedals, Hurst super shifter, and other interior detail.

the masking tape after a 20-minute soft cure. When you pull on the tape, the epoxy will try to stick to it and leave a textured appearance.

The interior is now ready for painting and detailing. I opted to flock the carpeting in the interior. The flocking will make a big mess, so try to work away from your workbench. Using a tacky craft glue and a salt shaker filled with flocking, I was able to get the result I desired.

Now I was ready to detail the interior. At this point you can scratchbuild a bench seat if you really want a neat street piece, or else you can glue in the kit bucket seats as I did. I added window cranks, which were missing, using S&S Specialties photoetch pieces from their interior detail kit. I added custom pedals from Detail Master to dress up the interior even more. I simulated the chrome door panel trim using Bare Metal foil, then paint detailed the instrument panel, attached under-dash gauges from Detail Master, and mounted a cable-driven tachometer from the parts box to the steering column. The cable for the tach drive was actually a silver Mylar thread used for fly-tying that I found in a sporting goods store. I detailed the steering wheel by adhering Bare Metal foil to the center section, trimming the foil

to the outermost edge of the center trim, painting the section flat black, and then buffing the high points of the trim—not a lot of work for a lot of added interior detail such as the double chrome trim and SS emblem. I found a great-looking Hurst super shifter with reverse lockout and line lock in Monogram's Rampage Camaro kit no. 2725. This was why I had removed the console.

The chassis needed minor modifications; specifically, I modified the frame rails for header side pipe clearance. I cut away the exhaust system from the differential and used Plastruct tubing to fill in the voids on the rear axle tubes where the stock exhaust pipes were molded in. I modified the kit's suspension risers to look more as if they belonged on the chassis instead of like bent pieces

of plastic, and they added lift to the rear of the car.

I used the big and little Goodyear tires supplied in the kit with one modification: I turned the tires inward and applied Shabo's Goodyear Polyglas lettering to the black wall side. The Shabo rub-ons are nice because they expand your tire choices, but they are a little tricky to use. Exact placement on the sidewall takes time and patience and, once applied, you need to do some cleanup around the letters. The tires now looked great, but they needed period wheels. Cragar wheels, from AMT/ERTL's 1966 Nova kit no. 6749, were a direct drop-in for the front tires. The rear tires needed a larger-diameter wheel, so I cut trim rings from two of the kit wheels and mated them to the Cragar

Spend the time to detail the dash—the results can be dramatic! Note the Detail Master underdash gauge cluster and the steering wheel detail.

When joined together, the interior bucket looks real.

Kit exhaust is molded to the rear axle tubes. With careful cutting and the addition of Plastruct tubing, removing the exhaust is clean and easy.

wheels. You can choose the depth, but make both trim rings the same. I cut short pieces of MSC black ignition wire and glued them into a hole in the mag rim to simulate valve stems. I painted the centers of the Cragar mags with Tamiya clear blue to add an extra bit of realism.

I tried something different with this project by painting and detailing the body first and assembling all the subassemblies, less the engine, together. I prepped and primed the body, then sprayed it with GM Bright Red, Plasticote no. 7104, directly from the can. I spent some time polishing out the paint with a polishing kit and with the Meguiar's liquid polishing system. I use this system on real cars and decided to try it on model cars—the results were outstanding!

Once the body was polished, I applied Bare Metal foil and epoxied the interior glass to the inside of the body. Use epoxy because plastic glue will eat into the roof over time and ruin it. I never tried super glue for this installation, so I can't comment on it.

The Chevelle glass came molded with rear side glass, and for added realism I ran a strip of $1/64''$ chrome stripping tape down the edge of both sides and painted the glass edge a semigloss black. This combination simulated the rubber and chrome strip on the car's side rear glass. I detailed the hood using decals from several Fred Cady sheets—the center stripe came from a 1969 Z/28 sheet no. 4, the outline stripe from a 1970 Corvette sheet no. 16, and the Motion emblem from Motion sheet no. 23. S&S Specialties photoetched hood pins replaced the molded ones. I made lanyards from silver wire strand that I fed through the glued clip, twisted, and then attached to the underside of the hood—and no, they do not actually work.

I thought I would try to build and detail the engine last and in the engine compartment; this kit

lent itself to this method since the entire front end is open. The kit engine is nice, but did not have a Lakewood scatter shield attached. The Rampage Camaro kit has a chromed unit that, when stripped and painted red, looks like the real thing. I cut the stock bell housing and transmission from the engine block. Be sure to cut material away from the bell housing and not the engine block. Once cut away, I sanded the engine block flat to accommodate the Lakewood bell housing. The Lakewood bell housing matches to the big block exactly. The Muncie four-speed from the Chevelle kit can be used if it is cut away from the stock bell housing, but I found it easier to grab one from the Rampage kit. If you do not have access to a Rampage kit, Scale Resin Detailers offers the bell housing in resin at a reasonable price.

I painted the engine block with Chevy orange, the heads with aluminum (of course), and the bell housing red. I painted the transmission case and the Edelbrock Torker manifold with aluminum. I had quite a time locating this manifold, and it was almost mandatory that I use one. Again, Scale Resin Detailers came to the rescue. When put

The kit suspension risers are cheesy, to say the least. You can achieve a more acceptable look by removing the L-shaped section of plastic.

I reversed the front tires, applied Shabo decals, and used a Cragar wheel from the AMT/ERTL 1966 Nova kit.

The rear tire needs a larger-diameter wheel rim. I achieved a deep-dish look by adding a trim ring cut from a Chevelle kit wheel and mating it to the Cragar mag.

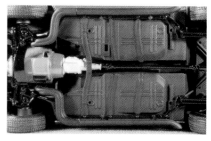

The new scatter shield attached. Note how the old unit was removed, and the amount of plastic remaining on the engine block. Also note the resin 780 CFM carb from Replicas and Miniatures and an air cleaner from a 1979 Monza kit. Also noteworthy is the resin Torker manifold from Scale Resin Detailers.

I laid the engine into the 90-percent-completed model. I enjoyed putting the final details on the engine in this manner. It was similar to working on a real car. Note all the details: Detail Master coil, Scale Resin Detailers MSD unit, and a Replicas and Miniatures Holley carb.

Side mount headers cleaned up the look of the chassis. Mounting brackets added to the side pipes' strength and allowed leveling.

together, the powertrain started to look like a performance unit.

The kit carburetor left a lot to be desired, but Replicas and Miniatures of Maryland offers the best-looking Holley 780 CFM carb in resin that I've ever seen. As small as this unit is, it is highly detailed and predrilled for fuel lines. I painted the carb with brass followed by a wash of Tamiya smoke to highlight some of the detail. I modified an S&S Specialties fuel filter to serve a dual purpose of fuel filter and double pumper fuel line. I cut a small section of wire from the fuel filter at one end and added it to the other end by the carb. With careful bending and placement it fit the Holley perfectly. I slid a no. 2 AN fitting from Detail Master over the wire nearest the back fuel bowl on the carb and positioned the small bent wire cut previously near the front fuel bowl. Once everything looked good, I tacked the fuel lines in place with super glue and slid the AN fitting over the joint. If this is your first time, this is a bit tricky and at times frustrating. To add to my frustration, I bent the fuel line and filter as one unit from the cool can to the back fuel bowl. It took me about

two hours of trial and error, but I did it—I will admit that it took two fuel filters to do it. Now, by painting select sections of wire flat black, you can achieve the appearance of fuel hose. Remember that back in the 1970s braided hose was found on airplanes, not on street cars. The Moroso cool can came from the Rampage kit, as well. While we're on the topic of the Rampage kit, I will add that it's a great kit for parts, if you're looking for vintage performance goodies.

I stripped the chrome from the cool can and painted it the appropriate colors (red lid and bottom) and used Humbrol flat hardened leather to simulate cork, a chrome silver lift knob, and 1/64″ chrome striping tape for the mounting strips. I use Mr. Clean to strip chrome. Used full strength, it strips chrome in a matter of minutes—about 30 minutes does it. The cool can is mounted to an indentation on the driver's side of the inner fender well in the final assembly. I set aside the fuel system for final fitting later, as well.

I used a prewired distributor from Parts by Parks, using yellow ignition wire to simulate Accel wires. I used S&S Specialties igni-

tion wire looms to clean up the look of the wired engine. I drilled the wire holes in the heads with a no. 75 X-acto drill bit and placed the wires in their proper firing order. I never used to do this, but found that when I did so the engine compartment looked better. Next, I permanently attached the carb and added a carb spring and tiny spring bracket. The carb spring is available from Randy Moyer, and I like his springs because they have a little extra wire at each end for attachment. The spring bracket was actually an S&S Specialties two-hole wire loom bent into an angle and attached to the front intake manifold bolt area. I bent a piece of MSC black ignition wire to resemble throttle linkage and attached it to the highly detailed carb throttle hardware. The Chevelle kit supplies an air conditioning fire wall condenser unit not normally found on Motion muscle cars. I needed a standard heater box and found it on a junked Monogram 1969 GTO body. I carefully cut the heater box away from the GTO's fire wall, sanded the unit thin, and glued it to the Chevelle fire wall. Once I was happy with all this detailing, I positioned the engine

Engine view with air cleaner off. Note the carb details, especially the butterflies.

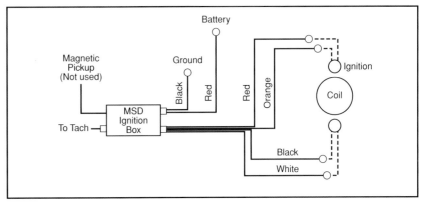

Street MSD ignition unit wiring diagram

in the bay and glued it in. I also did the final fitting of the fuel delivery system, heater hoses, and upper radiator hose. I paint detailed a Flexi-lite fan with aluminum and clear blue and glued it to the fan belt assembly. The kit alternator was huge, so I used a smaller unit from the parts box and glued that assembly to the front of the engine.

Other engine compartment detailing involved painting the washer bottle flat white and adding washer solvent with a blue highlighter. I painted the power brake booster with Testor's Metallizer brass—this is the most realistic brass color I have seen to date. I was sorry that I found out about it after I painted my Holley carb. The final details included a Detail Master machined aluminum coil and a Scale Resin Detailers MSD ignition box. I foiled the MSD unit on top, painted it flat red, and buffed the high spots to reveal the foil. I ran two wires from the MSD box heading toward the coil. I couldn't see actually wiring the unit, but if you want to, you'll find the wiring diagram for a street unit. MSD units were not offered in 1970, but showed up in the mid- to late 1970s. This was an owner-added option, for any purists out there who might take issue with this point. The ignition amplification unit used on 1970 Motion

cars was a Mallory unit—a brass-colored aluminum case with cooling fins and resistors on top.

Next I added the radiator support and shroud. I closed up the engine compartment, so now I could attach the upper radiator hose. I located a distinctive Motion-type air cleaner in my parts box; I believe it came from a 1979 Monza kit by MPC. I drilled into the air cleaner, but not through it, and glued a piece of wire into the drilled hole. The carb had a spot for a carb stud, so I drilled that out. The air cleaner now looked like a thumbtack and slid nicely into the hole in the carb, facilitating a removable air cleaner. I paint detailed all of the chrome body pieces and glued them in place. Then I painted the grille flat black with a body-colored center section. I also painted the rear bumper inserts flat black and detailed the SS emblems. Next, I painted all of the key locks with Tamiya silver paint. I placed a Chevelle decal from Fred Cady 1970 Chevelle sheet no. 22 on the right-hand side of the trunk lid. The molded-in Chevelle would have gotten lost in the paint, so I removed it prior to painting.

The last items I assembled were the side pipes. Monogram's 1966 Malibu Street Rat kit no. 2229 offers a set of header side

mounts for the big block. I wasn't sure that they would work, but from initial fittings I learned that they could work with some modification. I had notched the chassis earlier on in construction, so all I needed to do was modify the header units. I gently flattened the upper part of the area of the header where they begin to swoop back to the sewer pipes. This would be the mounting point of the header to the chassis frame rail and the strongest glue bond of the header system. The headers just plopped in perfectly when I test-fit them, so I applied super glue to two pipe ends at the head and to the flats of the pipes by the frame rails, and positioned them again perfectly. One pipe gave me trouble at the collector, since it was sitting at an angle. I carefully sanded the pipe square with a coarse sanding stick to give the remainder of the system a flush mating surface. Because of the length of the side pipe itself, I used four brackets from Ever-green strip and four isolator bushings from plastic rod. This gave the side pipes support and a firm mounting. The pipes can be leveled by adjusting the thickness of the isolator bushing.

I waxed the completed car with Meguiar's no. 26 carnuba wax, for added finish depth.

12
MOTION EMOTION
BUILDING A BALDWIN-MOTION 1968 CORVETTE

Growing up in Philadelphia in the late 1960s gave me many opportunities to get involved in the muscle car craze. To me, it meant friends who owned cars like GTOs, GTXs, Chevelles, Mustangs, Camaros, and of course Corvettes. If the truth must be known, I am a Vette freak. There's something about the lines of the car and the mystique surrounding it that really appeals to me. In the fall of 1968 I took a trip to New York to visit relatives. We managed to get into a heated debate over what the hottest cars were at the time. One thing led to another, and I soon found myself drooling at Baldwin Chevrolet in Long Island. There before me on the showroom floor was the most beautiful Vette I have ever seen: a Baldwin-Motion 427 coupe. These cars were special and were built for the not-so-faint of heart! The words "Baldwin-Motion" instilled fear on the street. The fabled Phase III engines started at 450 hp and went up to 600 hp—you could go as fast as your wallet would allow. Serious street racers owned Baldwin-Motion cars and were known to have hundred-dollar bills taped to their windshields.

Although I did not go for a ride on that day in 1968, in later years I did—and what a ride it was! You sit low in the cockpit. The engine thunders through the side pipes, and the bulging fenders remind you that you are in a special car. When the throttle is hammered, the car explodes with power. You are thrown deep into your seat as the secondaries kick

This chapter's photographs by Charles Cully

in. Second gear announces its presence with at least 30 feet of rubber. Those bulging fenders seem to lift as you tear down the road while the tachometer and speedometer needles bounce all over the instrument faces. These fabulous memories will last me a lifetime.

A few months ago, I happened to have a copy of a modeling magazine at work. A fellow employee in a department across the hall asked to see the issue, then asked me if I built models. When I replied yes, I was promptly commissioned to build a model for the department director as a surprise gift from the staff. At that time I only knew that it was a Corvette. I requested photos for the project and to my surprise, it turned out to be a 1968 Baldwin-Motion 427 Coupe. Needless to say, the project took on a new, emotional meaning for me. As I looked at the pictures, memories flooded into my mind of that day in 1968 on the show-

The detailed 1968 interior included keys, detailed instruments, and console detail.

room floor of Baldwin Chevrolet and of the day I drove a Baldwin-Motion Vette.

Baldwin-Motion cars came in many configurations—that's why there are cars with stripes and cars without. Money dictated options. If you sent for a Motion catalog in the late 1960s or early 1970s, you could order emblems, engines, or fiberglass to convert your own car. There were many Motion clones on the streets. This plastic conversion is a model of a cloned car that actually exists. When the real car was purchased from its previous owner, it had been restored with some modern "goodies" under the hood. Gone were the trademark SS 427 valve covers and unique air cleaner. So I built this model as an exact replica. I used seven kits for this special conversion. The major components were taken from Revell's 1969 Baldwin-Motion Corvette Coupe. Components from Revell's 1968 Corvette L-88 Roadster were used to convert the 1969 Coupe into a 1968. The following list is a breakdown of the kits used and the parts that were taken from these kits.

1. Revell 1969 Baldwin-Motion Corvette no. 7427: coupe body, side pipes, hood, basic components, and glass.
2. Revell 1968 L-88 Corvette Roadster no. 7159: interior parts and rear valance panel.
3. Revell No. 17 Superflo Camaro no. 7145: Moroso air cleaner and deep-dish trim rings.
4. Revell 427 Yenko Camaro no. 7132: intake manifold and carb.
5. Revell 1967 Malibu SS Pro Street no. 7147: Moroso valve covers.
6. ERTL 1966 Nova SS no. 6749: period-type Cragar mags.
7. I will mention this seventh kit later.

Prior to starting any project, remember to wash all raw plastic pieces in some type of dishwashing detergent such as Dawn. Paint, glue, and fillers will stick much better to a clean plastic surface. Do not wash the chrome pieces, as the chrome may wash off.

The 1969 Coupe body needed to be back-dated to a 1968. I accomplished this by cutting away the rear valance panel with the back of a no. 11 X-acto blade.

Other details included great-looking photoetched sunglasses from S&S Specialties and a photoreduced copy of *Vette* magazine, available from Scale Vanities.

Then I did the same to the 1968 Roadster body. If these cuts are made carefully, the 1968 panel fits the 1969 body perfectly. As a bonus, the 1969 panel also fits the 1968 roadster body—ah, another conversion project to think about! I also needed the remove the lock from and dimple the 1969 door. I used a drill bit the same diameter as the door lock to recess a place for the 1968 lock button. Be careful not to drill completely through the door. Then I used a slightly larger drill bit to radius the recess. I looked at reference material to approximate the size of the door lock button dimple.

Wheel well flares on the model are subtle but very much part of the body. To accomplish this, I used mud flaps found in the original issue MPC 1973 Roadrunner kit—the seventh kit. I'm sure dealers and collectors are falling over right about now! For a substitute, you can use sheet plastic cut and shaped to the Corvette body. For a stronger bond to the body, you need to remove a portion the thickness of the mud flap from the wheel lip. This allows the flap to be

mounted flush to the wheel lip on the inside.

Once I had glued all four flaps to the body and allowed them to dry, I used polyester glazing compound to blend the flap into the body. A small round file can be used to give the back of the flare a curvature; rolled-up sandpaper will work too. The diameter of the sandpaper will determine the amount of curvature. Polyester glazing compound is great to work with—it sets up in about half an hour and can be sanded easily. It will not bleed through the paint, nor will it crack as time goes by. I removed the mold lines from the body, then sanded it smooth and corrected any defects. The Revell body was basically quite clean.

I applied Tempo sandable primer and completely wet-sanded the body, then applied another coat of sandable primer. After the body was cleaned and dry, I sprayed on a coat of non-sandable primer. I used the LMG Enterprises Micro Gloss sanding kit extensively in this project, and the final results were worth it. I applied flat red as a base for the color coat, sanding each primer coat with a 6000-grit polishing cloth.

I airbrushed a custom paint mix onto the body, consisting of Testor's kiln red metallic with about 15 drops of Testor's stoplight red metallic. I applied four coats of this custom mix. I applied a final "kiss-coat" of color mixed with Testor's clear gloss for added gloss. I sanded the body after each coat of color with an 8000-grit polishing cloth and rubbed it initially with no. 5 Meguiar's glaze after the first two color coats, then no. 7 Meguiar's glaze after the final coats. Meguiar's no. 5 and no. 7 glazes can be applied to the painted surface to remove roughness, blemishes, or light orange peel. The beauty of this product is that it is paintable—you can apply successive coats of paint over the polished surface. Gentle manipulation is a must, otherwise the polish will cut through the paint to the primer. These steps yielded a very high gloss finish. I applied a final "kiss-coat" of Testor's clear gloss and let dry. I set aside the body to dry thoroughly while I assembled the chassis, engine, and interior.

I sprayed the interior flat black. I used the dash and door panels from the 1968 Roadster kit, painting the details with Testor's chrome silver—including the shift pattern on the console. I painted the dash gauge details flat white and coated them with Micro Krystal Kleer to simulate lenses. For an added detail feature, I mixed the Krystal Kleer with a drop of dilute Tamiya clear green to give the instruments that Chevy green look. I also added other details at this time. I epoxied keys from S&S Specialties (now Detail Resources) to the dash (remember, it's a 1968). I glued a photo-reduced copy of *Vette* magazine, available from Scale Vanities, to the passenger seat and a laid a pair of photoetched sunglasses, also from S&S, on top of the magazine. If you buy nothing else this year, you must get these sunglasses—the instructions show you how to make lenses using Tamiya smoke acrylic paint. It was incredibly easy to do, and added so much to the interior. I set aside the interior for installation later.

I built the chassis box stock. I painted it my trademark flat black with gloss frame rails and hardware. Chrome-plated front springs were supplied in the kit. I painted flat black between the coils and gave it a quick wipe with thinner on the raised portion of the coil to remove excess paint, which yields a nice-looking coil spring that pops out when buried in the front suspension A arms. I set the completed chassis aside to dry thoroughly.

I assembled the engine block with the heads, manifold, and water pump and painted the unit with Testor's Chevy engine orange. I painted the bell housing with Lakewood red and the transmission with polished steel. I tacked the carburetor and air cleaner to the manifold and laid engine into the chassis, then test-fitted it into the body with the hood down. I encountered clearance problems, so I needed to trim the frame mounts on the chassis to lower the engine. This was a trial-and-error fitting. This lowering of the engine needs to be carried over into the rest of the engine compartment assembly later. Once I had determined the correct engine height, I could wire the engine, detail it, and glue the rest of the parts. I used Detail Master blue ignition wire to simulate Moroso wire. The real car's engine used the ignition shielding, but without the side arms. I cut a resin copy of Monogram's 1965 Black Rat Vette air cleaner to free the shielding from the air cleaner. I drilled the shielding for wires, then painted it with polished steel, buffed it, and used Plastruct tubing to mount it to the top of the intake manifold. I routed ignition wire from both sides of the shielding and into appropriate spark plug locations between exhaust manifold ports—I used exhaust manifolds from the kit and painted them gunmetal. I epoxied Detail Master T-valve cover bolts into holes drilled into the Moroso big block valve covers. At this time I permanently attached the carburetor and air cleaner.

Engine detail abounds with photoetched T-valve cover bolts, braided hoses, and AN fittings. All details were matched to engine pictures of the real car.

I used braided fuel line from the fuel pump to the double-pumper carb, which I found difficult to work with. Once the hose was cut, it tended to fray before I could insert it into an AN fitting. The cutting process tended to flatten the hose, and in tight spots the hose was not very flexible. When it came time to do the radiator hose, I ran into some of the same problems. I found chrome Mylar braided string was at—of all places—L.L. Bean's fishing department! Any well-equipped sporting goods store that carries fly-making supplies will carry this string. There were several diameters to choose from, and it was easy to work with. Once I had cut it with a sharp blade, I placed a drop of epoxy on the cut end to prevent the hose from fraying prior to installation.

Final engine/chassis placement can take place once the engine has completely dried. Once I had finished all of the engine fitting, I glued the engine into the chassis. I attached remaining hardware such as the pulleys, belts, alternator, and fan to the engine. I glued the radiator, support, and fan shroud to the chassis. The radiator support piece, once installed, was too tall and interfered with the hood. It would not allow the hood to sit flush with the fenders. It should be trimmed from the top prior to installation.

The taillights were custom red lenses, available in the model railroad section of well-equipped hobby shops.

Wheels and tires were also special. See the text for assembly instructions.

I epoxied the glass to the inside of the body and the rearview mirror to the windshield in its proper place. Then I brush-painted the entire inside of the body with flat black. I test-fitted taillight bezels and epoxied red railroad MV lenses into the taillight bezels. Then I epoxied the completed light assembly into the appropriate openings in the rear of the body. I also glued the license plate frame to the rear of the body, from the inside. The rear kit glass was curved, which is a minor inaccuracy—the rear glass is straight on the real car.

Then I glued the fender wells in place according to the kit instructions. Even with extensive trimming of the hood and its opening, the hood was difficult to open. On the first attempt, the paint chipped slightly. This was upsetting, to say the least! I cut off the hinge pins, since they appeared to cause the fit problem. I used short, modified straight pins as replacement hinge points. The pins are held by friction and would be pushed through the hinge mounts in the engine compartment during the final assembly step. I friction-fit the fire wall into the body until the interior was placed and permanently attached. I needed to remove a

portion of the vacuum canister from the fire wall so that it would clear the valve covers in the engine bay. Then I epoxied the completed interior in place. Once this was accomplished, I slid the fire wall into place and epoxied it. Epoxy was the preferred adhesive, as it will not damage the body as time passes.

Now came the tricky part: installing the chassis. Correctly aligning all the parts in the body makes chassis installation easier. It was a precarious installation, as I had just one chance to snap in the chassis without causing any damage to the painted body. One of the mounting pins was misaligned and would not allow the chassis to snap correctly in place. A little surgical excision of excess plastic allowed the chassis to eventually snap in correctly. I could only accomplish chassis installation without the wheels and tires mounted to the chassis. Then I mounted the chrome bumpers to the body. I used flat black wash on the front grille and painted the parking lights flat white with a tiny dot of Tamiya clear orange to represent an amber bulb. I used Bare Metal foil on the side marker lights, then painted the front lenses as I had the front parking lights. I also used Bare Metal foil on the

rear backup lights and painted them flat white. I used Fred Cady decals, sheet no. 16, for the 427 and Stingray scripts. These scripts have been revised on newer decals sheets and now appear in silver. Older sheets provided these scripts in white.

I detailed Goodyear big and little tires, from the Monogram 1970 Chevelle kit, by outlining the raised outline letters with flat white. Standard offset Cragar mags fit comfortably into the front tires. A custom feature was the body color I added to the center caps. I used Detail Master wire to represent a valve stem in the wheel. The rear wheels were too small for the opening in the tire and bottomed out inside the tire. This situation lends itself to a deep-dish mag. I found a trim ring the same diameter as the tire opening in a race car kit, Revell's no. 17 Dynaflo Camaro, and fitted it to the tire, then sanded it to achieve the correct depth. I scraped the outside edge of the mag rim of chrome, inside the tire, to provide a good glue joint for the new trim ring. I also added valve stems to the rear wheels. Then I added the completed wheel and tire assemblies to the body. Fortunately, they fit perfectly.

Final detailing included adding a door mirror, mounted with Detail Master wire used as a dowel. Door lock buttons were two-piece photoetched items from the S&S Specialties shapes pack. I added photoreduced license plates from Scale Vanities to the front and back of the car. I added a photoetched license plate frame to the front plate and an S&S Specialties radio antenna to the rear deck. Note that S&S Specialties no longer carries this item—what a pity! The last details I added were photoetched Corvette crossed flags. I detailed

If cut correctly, the rear valance from the 1968 roadster looks as if it is molded to the 1969 body.

The door needs only a gentle dimple for the door lock button.

A closer look at the flare detail shows that the flares are not radical, but definitely there.

the flags with Tamiya clear red and hand-painted the checkered pattern with flat black. I attached the photoetched parts with epoxy. I've had poor results in past experience using super glue. White residue on the paint or the photoetched parts has always been the plague of super glue. Epoxy is forgiving in that it dries clear and gives the builder a chance to position parts. Excess epoxy removes easily with Bare Metal plastic polish.

I ran Tamiya acrylic smoke into all the body joints for color contrast. I find that flat black looks too unrealistic. The vacuum canister and master cylinder had

to be modified to fit over the taller Moroso valve cover. Both units were, basically, notched for clearance. I put the notch on the underside so that it would not be noticeable when viewed from outside the engine compartment. Once everything was in place in the engine compartment, I could place the hood. I pushed out the two 1/4˝ straight pins used to replace the molded plastic pins once the hood was aligned with the hinge holes in the inner fender wells. Trial opening of the hood went very easily, and no more paint chipping occurred.

I gently polished the entire car with Micro Gloss polish, using a cotton swab. After buffing it, I applied two coats of Meguiar's no. 26 yellow wax in the same fashion and buffed again. The result was an as-advertised, mirror-gloss finish.

I mounted the car to a custom wood base using straight pins that were placed into the sanded tire tread, then positioned it into drilled holes in the wood base. This method of mounting is very

clean and secure—there are no wires or rubber bands to spoil the effect of the model.

The overall fit and finish of the model was good. I encountered several problems in the engine compartment, though. Even though I lowered the engine quite a bit, the fan blade still appeared to be a fraction above the fan shroud. The steering box was such a tight fit that, even with trimming, I found it easier to leave it out of the assembly process. This omission proved to be helpful later when I installed the chassis.

I had the pleasure of presenting the finished model at work. I am always reluctant to give up a finished project, and this was no exception. I had put 175 hours into the model and spent about $116.00 on kits and extra parts. When the director uncovered his gift, he was speechless. The look in his eyes made parting with the model easier—I knew it would go to a good home. It was an emotional moment—or you could say, "Motion emotions!"

13

HOW BUICK STAGED AN ELEPHANT HUNT

BUILDING RICHARD LASSETER'S 1970 BUICK GS 455 STAGE 1

Underhood detail was taken to the max.

I have always had a soft spot in my heart for Buicks. In high school I saved all my pocket change and the money I earned mowing lawns, putting it in a jar labeled "GSX FUND," after I saw an ad for the 1970 GSX. So naturally, I was thrilled when Monogram released the kit. Not only could I build a GSX, but I could also build Richard Lasseter's 1970 Buick GS Stage 1, pictured on the cover of *Car Review*. I wrote a letter to the Buick GS Club stating my intentions and requesting detailed information. I was pleasantly surprised to receive a reply from Richard Lasseter himself. He was more than gracious, supplying me with lots of information and several Buick Club license plates for my project. We exchanged several letters, and he eventually persuaded me to build a replica of his own car for him. I contacted Mark Budniewski of MPB Detail Products to discuss options for the GS emblems, since he was contemplating producing these emblems for sale. My original plan was to use the kit decals and make the grille

clear red. Richard's Buick had hood pins, which I had originally planned on making functional. I figured that once he received the car he would have the hood off often, so owing to the delicate nature of photo-etched parts, I mounted the four-piece hood pin to the top of the hood and secured it to the underside. The S&S Specialties hood pin kit provides the scuff plate and the clip. I drilled a small hole to match the size of the needle used for the post and eyelet. I accomplished this by attaching the scuff plate, drilling the center hole, and gluing in the top of the needle eye. I used epoxy to attach photoetched parts, since super glue tends to frost. I pulled two wire fibers from insulated wire to serve as the hood pin cables and twisted it using a toothpick—this method gives a nice twist and a perfect loop. Be sure to use a round toothpick. The further up the toothpick shaft you go, the larger the loop will be. I threaded the S&S hood pin clip through the loop, then clipped it into the eye of the needle. I placed a minute drop of epoxy to hold the clip in the eye of the needle. I routed the free end of the cable to the underside of the hood and secured it. You may think this was a lot of trouble, but the end result will leave you speechless! Other interior details came from Scale Vanities: a photoreduced copy of the March 1985 issue of *Car Review* magazine, a "CAR REVIEW" plate, and 1970 Buick GSX model box. The quality of these custom pieces was great and added much to the model. In the parts box, I found a screwdriver and painted it to resemble a Stanley brand tool.

Here is the passenger-side frame notch for header tube clearance. This will vary with your choice of headers.

Here is the driver's side frame notch for header tube clearance.

This left the GS and Stage 1 emblems. MPB Detail Products outdid itself with this little-known item. The scripts were so nice, they could be considered fine jewelry. They came with detailed instructions for painting and mounting. The instruction sheet provides placement dimensions, so I will not bother to mention them here. I painted the red with Tamiya clear red and the black with Testor's flat black. Initially I was concerned about the front grille GS emblem and how it would cover the molded-in GSX emblem. MPB did their homework, because the GS emblem nearly covered the old one completely. If you are even remotely considering a Buick GS project, by all means get these emblems.

This photo shows the roof molding placement for a two-tone color or a vinyl top application.

MPB Detail Products makes the beautiful photoetched GS and Stage 1 emblems. They are a must for this project!

I carefully rubbed down the entire car with Bare Metal plastic polish, then waxed it with Meguiar's no. 26 wax—my personal favorite.

This was the most ambitious project I had ever built. The question everyone asks me is how I was able to part with this model since I spent 160 hours over a period of a year to construct it. The model was personalized so much that I felt that it did not belong to me, even though I built it. Richard was very much into this project, as I was into his car. This project gave me a real sense of gratification by testing my abilities to the limit. The other often-asked question was how much I charged Richard for the model. All I'll say is that his friendship is payment enough.

COLOR GALLERY

1969 Yenko SC 427 Camaro. Photo by Charles Cully.

The heart of the beast! Yenko's 427-cubic-inch fire-breather, rated at 450 horse-power. Photo by Charles Cully.

1969 Pontiac GTO Ram Air IV Judge

1970 Chevrolet Monte Carlo SS454

This Monte Carlo SS454 is a replica of a real car owned by Mary Jane Godino.

This highly modified 454-cubic-inch engine has wire and hose detail along with custom wire looms, MSD box, and coil.

1968 Pontiac GTO 400

1970 Baldwin-Motion Phase III Chevelle

1970 Oldsmobile 442 W-30

1990 25th anniversary Mustang LX convertible. The real car was owned by Carol Kish.

The Mustang interior was detailed with a host of photoetched and photoreduced items. Note the cassette on the console and the window sticker on the seat!

The engine compartment was detailed with kit parts to represent the potent Mustang 5.0 engine.

A closer view of the interior also shows keys in the ignition as well as an automatic shifter.

1968 Baldwin-Motion 427 Phase III Corvette. The real car, which is not a Baldwin-Motion car but a clone, is currently owned by Harry Polsky, M.D. Special-effect photography by Charles Cully.

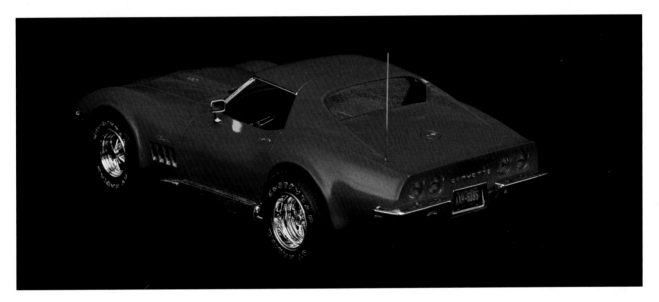

A rear view of the model shows off the custom taillights. Special-effect photography by Charles Cully.

1986 Monte Carlo SS454. Special-effect photography by Charles Cully.

The heart of the "Humbler," a modified
455-cubic-inch engine

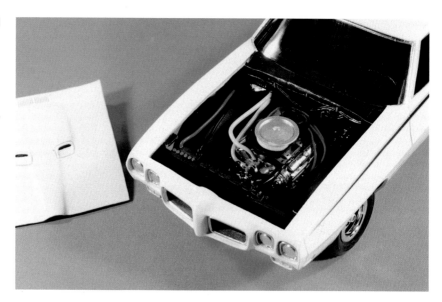

1970 Pontiac GTO 455 c.i.d., affectionately called "The Humbler"

1971 Plymouth 'Cuda 440 6-pack

The 1971 440 6-pack with chrome dress-up parts, nestled in the 'Cuda's engine compartment

1971 Plymouth Hemi GTX

The strobe stripes, GTX graphics, and wide rear tires capture the '70s muscle car era in plastic.

The Hemi was detailed with wires and chrome.

1970 Buick GS Stage 1, modeled after Richard Lasseter's own "ol' Blue." Richard dubbed the model "li'l Blue."

The Buick 455 Stage 1 kit engine was heavily detailed to resemble the real engine. Note the wires, fuel filter, air cleaner, and even antifreeze in the overflow bottle. Also note the photoetched emblems on the side of the front fender!

1970 Dodge Superbee

The Dodge Superbee is painted in Plum Crazy with one of three stripe variations.

1969 Plymouth Roadrunner 440 6-pack

1974 Plymouth Hemi Duster. Model built by Tom Buesgen.

The car looks docile, but under the hood lurks mega horsepower in the form of a modified Hemi. The only tipoff is the "HEMI" emblem on the front fender.

14
STREET SURVIVOR
FOIL AND EPOXY EMBLEMS FOR A 1974 HEMI DUSTER

In the mid- to late 1970s the muscle car craze had pretty much died out—the insurance companies, oil companies, and Detroit saw to that. The most "muscular" offerings from Detroit were "disco" T/A Firebirds and lukewarm Camaro Zs. This left many true die-hard muscle car lovers out in the cold. To survive, many built their own powerhouses. Engine swapping was very popular and made for many interesting street pieces. V-8 Vegas and Pintos were common, as were Hemi-powered Mopar products. All that horsepower had to be tamed with a decent suspension, and the wildest combinations of engines and bodies made it to the streets. These radical street pieces were primarily

responsible for today's Pro-Street scene. The dyed-in-the-wool street racers went for tire-smokin' street power, in any form.

Tom Buesgen, one of my "basement buddies," captured the feel of that era with his Hemi-powered 1974 Duster. This Plum Crazy street piece is the epitome of what was common. MPC's 1974 Duster kit was the basis for this build-up, and the Hemi engine even came in the kit— which tells you where the kit manufacturers' minds were. The engine compartment in Tom's Duster was heavily detailed with yellow Accel ignition wire from Detail Master, wire looms from Detail Resources, an Accel Super Coil from Performance Detail Parts, a single four-barrel carbu-

retor and intake setup, and a Moroso air cleaner. These were all state-of-the-art performance parts back then. He paint detailed the interior and added a Hurst shifter along with dashtop gauges. He built the chassis with a slight rake, which was common to cars of that era. He painted the body with Plum Crazy, acrylic enamel, polished with an 8000-grit polishing cloth and polishing cream—both from LMG Enterprises—and waxed with Meguiar's no. 26 yellow wax. Other details included Scale Vanities license plates, period Cragar mags, and Goodyear white-lettered tires. He made foil and epoxy 426 emblems and added them to the fenders to give this sleeper some character.

Meguiar's liquid polishes are available in automotive supply stores. Pictured here are no. 2 fine cut cleaner, no. 9 scratch and swirl remover, and no. 7 show car glaze.

Novus plastic polish is available as a two-part kit—one bottle has cleaner and the other contains a clear liquid polish.

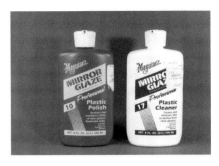

Meguiar's also has a two-step plastic cleaner and polish.

Top off your polishing project with the Wax Shop super glaze for an ultra-wet-looking finish!

Here is a "before" shot of my 1957 Chevy, built in 1973. I painted this model with GM touchup lacquer paint and never finished it properly. After 20-plus years, I will treat it to a proper finish!

How's that for shine? I subjected the roof to the process discussed in the text. Note how it compares to the trunk lid.

tried Bare Metal polish and it brought back the shine and depth with just one application. I have also found that Bare Metal polish works great with the new Boyd's colors from Testor's.

Novus Plastic Polish and Meguiar's Plastic Polish

Both of these products are designed to work well on acrylic surfaces. Again, on the new Boyd's color from Testor's, these products will enhance the color and shine of the finish. Additionally, automotive acrylic finishes come alive with one application of this two-step process. Urethanes will also respond well.

Novus comes as a two-step kit. The no. 2 cleaner is a milky tan solution that goes on easily and puts down a shine almost immediately. I found that it took many applications to remove orange peel, and I suggest using either a fine-grit sanding cloth or the Meguiar's no. 2 to start. Novus no. 1 is a clear liquid that goes on easily, fogs up when dry, and buffs to a high gloss.

Meguiar's plastic polish is also a two-step process—one step is a cleaner and the other a fine polish. I have used these steps after the previously mentioned Meguiar's steps but prior to final waxing. Meguiar's products are basically a series of finer and finer grits of polishing liquid. Both the cleaner and the polish are milky tan consistency, go on easily, and buff off easily.

All plastic polishes can be used on bare plastic. This is especially nice for promos, snap kits, or even glue kits that will never see a coat of paint. Painting over Novus or Meguiar's plastic polish is not mentioned on either product label and should be construed as not recommended.

16
A GIFT HORSE
BUILDING THE 25TH ANNIVERSARY MUSTANG CONVERTIBLE

People who know me realize that this type of project is totally out of character for me. I usually build late 1960s and early 1970s muscle machines. But my brother-in-law convinced me to build a 25th anniversary 1990 Mustang LX convertible so that he could present it as a gift to someone who owned the real car. At first I was a bit apprehensive, since Fords are not my area of expertise and this project would be a late model car. As I started the project, I became very interested in it. The model went together easily, and this conversion became a pleasurable experience. I will admit, though, that it almost didn't take place. I needed a 1990s-style nose piece and taillights, possibly cast in resin. I sent letters to the various resin casters asking for assistance with this project. The return letters were a bit discouraging in that no one could help

Pictured here are the kits used in this 25th Anniversary Mustang conversion.

me out. My last hope was Art Anderson from All American Models. I sent out my desperate plea, and within a few days he responded by phone. He could help me out with the nose piece, but I was on my own with the taillights. My thanks goes to Art for his help in this project. Now I was

ready to begin the conversion.

I used the following Monogram kits: the 1983 Mustang convertible no. 2222 supplied the body, taillights, and windshield; the 1989 Mustang convertible no. 2911 supplied the wheels and detail parts; and the 1992 Mustang convertible no. 2953 supplied the

I used the All American Models LX Mustang coupe for its nose piece.

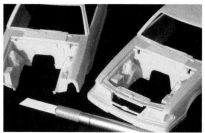

Before and after the cut. The resin nose would be used on the modified 1983 Mustang convertible body.

All I needed to do was remove these two body pieces to modify the 1983 body to accept the 1990 nose.

interior, engine, chassis, and the well-detailed trunk rack. All American Models supplied the LX coupe body. I removed the exclusive LX nose for grafting to the 1983 convertible body. I was asked why I would destroy a perfectly good resin body just for its nose. The body I sacrificed was an imperfect body that Art would not sell, but it was perfect for my purposes.

I needed to remove the mirror mounts from the sides of the 1983 convertible kit body and file the sides of the windshield moldings to match. Then I drilled new mirror mounts into the door. The 1990s body can be used as a guide for placement of the mounting hole. I removed the Mustang LX emblem on the left side of the trunk lid and left the Ford blue oval on the right side. Then I removed the original nose piece by running a no. 11 X-acto blade along the distinct division between the trim and the fender, starting with the headlight surround pieces. I made the cuts generously, leaving enough material to sand and fit the new nose into.

I also removed the engine compartment at this time. The 1990s engine compartment had the battery mounted on the opposite side. This removal sounds worse than it actually was. I carefully removed the 1983

engine compartment using a small X-acto saw blade, again cutting generously so that sanding and final fitting could be accomplished. A new engine compartment from a 1990s body would be grafted in as a replacement. When cut properly, the engine compartment and radiator shroud resemble a U. I made many careful trial-and-error fittings and did the final attachment with super glue. I flipped over the 1983 body and located the two interior mounting pins under the cowl vent, removing these pins, since the newer interior had its mounting points set wider apart. I used trial-and-error fitting to attain a flush fit. I filed two notches into the outside area of the convertible boot mechanism bays.

Now, working with the resin body, I cut away the nose piece. Again I used generous cuts, anticipating sanding and fitting later. You can always sand material away for fit, but it's more difficult to add material if you have cut away too much. On a cautionary note, resin sands into a very fine dust that can be irritating to some people. Be sure to wear a mask when working with resin if you are predisposed to these problems. Once the nose was fitted, I glued it to the 1983 body with super glue. If by chance you make an error in fit-

ting, use super glue debonder and start over.

The Ford oval in the resin grille was supported by a very thin and fragile bar. I reinforced this with a straight pin cut to fit the back of the bar. The pin should be slightly longer than the resin bar, bent to follow the contour and mounted to the solid resin area behind the headlight bucket. I held the reinforcement in place with five-minute epoxy and set it aside to dry. This combination gave the trim piece considerable strength and durability for sanding and shaping later.

Then I sanded the body with 800-grit sandpaper, washed it, dried it, and sprayed it with Tempo sandable primer. Then I sanded the dry, primed body smooth with a finer sanding cloth and washed it again. I sprayed the body with regular primer, allowed it to dry, sanded it smooth, and washed it once more. This time I was careful when sanding not to sand through the primer. I set the body aside to fully dry and wait for the paint. The paint was mixed at a local auto body supply shop, using Dupont Centari acrylic enamel code PA, deep Jewel Green Metallic. I applied the paint with an airbrush in light coats, sanding after each coat had dried. Don't forget to

I needed to remove the mirror mounts and file the windshield molding to match the length of the windshield frame.

Pictured here is the fragile resin Ford nose bar.

You can and should reinforce the nose bar with a steel pin and epoxy. Cut the pin slightly longer than the resin bar. When dry, this assembly yields a solid bar that will take some abuse from sanding or handling without breaking.

paint the mirrors—it's best to paint them off the body and attach them with epoxy to the predrilled mounting points on the doors after they are completely dry. Once the paint was applied to the body and completely dry, I rubbed it out with Meguiar's no. 5 and no. 7 glazes. This left the finish jewel-like. I performed final waxing later using Meguiar's no. 26 carnuba wax. I masked off the areas to be painted matte black. My personal choice for a matte finish is to use Testor's flat black followed with an overcoat of semigloss clear. Remember to let the paint dry fully before attempting to mask any parts. In addition, be sure to use only a good-quality masking tape. My preference is any 3M product. In the past I tried using bargain tape, but found the results were poor—I had paint bleeding problems and

lots of masking residue left on a painted surface. In a few instances I even lost my finish to a strong adhesive on the tape that pulled the paint off the surface of the plastic. When the body was completely painted and dry, I glued the windshield, with the rearview mirror attached, into its proper location.

I painted the chassis body color, and built box stock it abounded with detail. I painted front and rear suspension pieces a semigloss black, which contrasted nicely with the emerald green floor pans of the chassis. I painted the exhaust with a buffing stainless steel and brought it to a highly reflective luster when dry. I would add exhaust tips in the final detailing steps. My preference was to use 1/8″ aluminum tubing for the tail pipe extensions. I took wheels from Monogram kit no. 2911 and detailed

them by flowing matte aluminum paint between the raised ribs of the wheel. I also added valve stems to the wheels for an extra bit of realism, using MSC black ignition wire. A suitable substitute can be found in the Detail Master catalog. When the wire is cut, a small amount of bare metal is exposed, which resembles the actual metal screw top found on a real valve stem. I sanded the tire tread to depict wear. I built the engine box stock, using matte aluminum on the intake and valve covers as depicted on the real car. I modified the manual transmission to resemble an automatic unit. I used the kit under-hood decals, which really added to the realism of the engine compartment. I achieved the rest of the under-hood detail by using different colors and metallic shades of paint.

I took the interior from the 1992 Mustang kit. I needed to remove the interior console arm rest and sand the area smooth. Since my version was an automatic, I removed the clutch pedal and scratchbuilt the shifter and shift indicator. I made the console insert for the shift indicator from clear Evergreen, which I fitted in the shifter hole. I drilled out a slot for shift travel and carefully shaped it. I then made the

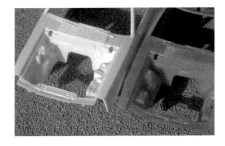

Engine compartment comparison of 1983 (right) to 1990 (left). This swap is essential.

With careful cutting, the old engine compartment can be removed so that you can graft a newer one in its place. Patience and careful cutting and fitting will give you a clean swap.

Once the resin nose is grafted and painted, it's hard to tell that it's not part of the original kit. Note the reflective quality of the headlights.

This close-up photo of the rear shows the taillight detail, luggage rack, tail pipes, and photoreduced license plate.

shifter from a bent straight pin and a handle I found in the parts box. I paint detailed the rest of the interior with white for the seats, door panels, and the lower part of the dash. I painted the top of the dash with Testor's Euro I gray, then painted the carpeting and the lower portion of the door panels a slightly lighter shade, dark gull gray. I put semigloss on the painted interior to give it the appearance of vinyl. Detail pictures were a great help here—I encourage you to take as many pictures as possible when building replica stock models. I personally feel that this category of model is extremely difficult, since every detail must be replicated exactly as it appears on the real car.

I detailed the gauges and controls right down to the red and blue on the temperature control knob for the heater. I added keys and the ignition switch from Detail Resources as well as a cassette tape, which I placed on the console as if it were laid there by the driver. I applied the kit window sticker decal to a sheet of wrapping tissue and allowed it to dry and wrinkle. As this dried it was

trimmed. After it dried, I glued it to the front seat, and it had the appearance of a sticker that had just been removed by the dealer. The back seat sported two issues of *Mustang Monthly* magazine, one of which was a 25th anniversary issue. These photoreduced items were obtained from Scale Vanities.

The interior, body, and chassis went together very easily—it was almost scary! The model was now ready for final detailing. Starting with the body, I applied Bare Metal foil to the area where the taillights would mount. I took the taillights from the 1983 convertible kit and detailed them using Tamiya clear red X-27, clear orange X-26, Testor's flat black, and Chart-Pack tape. Then I epoxied these detailed units to the areas of Bare Metal foil on the rear panel. Be sure to use just enough glue to attach it, and not so much that it oozes out from behind the lens. Silver dry transfer lettering supplied the new LX emblem. I detailed the Ford blue oval with Bare Metal foil and Tamiya clear blue X-23. This combination made the emblem look very realistic. I detailed the fender 5.0 emblems with Bare

Metal foil as well, and painted the dot with Testor's fluorescent red. I painted the parking lights on the headlight lenses with Tamiya clear orange X-26 and set them aside for the moment. I painted the headlight buckets with polished steel and buffed them. Then I painted the outer edge of the bucket flat black. I applied a very fine bead of epoxy to this edge and plopped the lens onto the wet epoxy. I did this in one quick motion so that I didn't smear glue onto the lens. If you move the lens around, you risk smearing the glue all over the lens. Backing clear lenses with a reflective metallic background makes the lights appear to be very realistic. I prefer to use Bare Metal for flat surfaces and a buffing aluminum or steel for areas with compound curves.

I painted the trunk rack matte black and glued it to the deck lid. I also painted a Detail Resources radio antenna (no longer available) matte black and mounted it in a small hole I previously drilled out on top of the passenger-side front fender near the cowl. For final crowning touches, I added a front "First Pennsylvania Mustang Club"

Interior detail reveals magazines, keys in the ignition, a dealer window sticker, and a cassette tape on the console.

The automatic shifter is another subtle detail.

The engine was an absolute joy to assemble and looks right at home in the transplanted engine compartment.

plate and a Pennsylvania "SAMPLE" tag in back. The rear tag was only temporary until the owner's real tag could be photoreduced.

The kit supplied an up-top and a convertible boot. I painted both pieces with Testor's flat white and overcoated them with semigloss. I did not permanently attach the boot or up-top, so that they could be interchanged as desired. The extensively detailed interior obviously shows better with the convertible boot option.

A project that I was originally apprehensive about turned out to be quite rewarding and fun. The success of my projects usually depends on my interest in the particular subject. This model project renewed my interest and enthusiasm in modern muscle cars. Granted, these cars won't plant your molars into the back of your throat, but there is certainly new excitement with each curve in the road.

17
SOPHISTICATED RODENT

CONVERTING MONOGRAM'S 1986 MONTE CARLO SS INTO A FANTASY

My wife and I live in a small suburban town in Pennsylvania. It's a quiet little town famous for a college, a smorgasbord, and fantastic pizza. The kids that attend the college are pretty decent and as rowdy as college kids can be. One Saturday night I was waiting for a pizza and happened to be sitting near a group of guys from one of the dorms. As I waited, a college guy walked in and announced to his buddies that he had just finished working on his new Monte Carlo SS. He proudly boasted that it was now one awesome piece of machinery. One of his friends asked what he had done, and he replied, "I put in a hi-po computer chip. It took me all afternoon, and let me tell you, that beast really flies!" It took every ounce of restraint I had not to break out laughing—the guy hardly got his hands dirty, and there he is boasting about his "beast." Unfortunately, he was too young to know the true meaning of the word. He apparently never drove a late 1960s muscle car to know what brutal performance was, nor did he ever experience the power and torque of a big block Chevy at full throttle. I could just imagine his face if his Monte had a big block! With this thought the idea for this conversion was born.

Imagine the year 1989 with no insurance regulations, no pollution restrictions, and automakers building the cars of the 1960s and 1970s using modern body styles and technologies. You walk into a Chevy dealer's showroom, pick up a Monte Carlo brochure, and rush home to study it in great detail. You open the book to find a beautiful Steel Cities Gray Monte SS 454 pictured, and the caption below the picture reads,

"Cardiac Arrest!" The goosebumps start to form as you read the following: "New for 1989, the LS-5 option transforms your already powerful Monte Carlo SS into a heart-stopping performer! The 454-cubic-inch LS-5 standard

Here is the completed big block, ready for service. Note the use of the serpentine belt and assorted accessories.

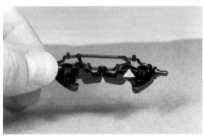

The front K member is notched at the arrows to accommodate the oil pan and starter.

engine delivers 360 horsepower to handle any performance requirements but is tame enough for daily driving with its 8.5 compression ratio. The M-22 standard four-speed and 3.73 12-bolt rear act as liaison between the power and the pavement! A Turbo 400 automatic is available. Other standard features include a 2.5-inch true dual exhaust system, power disc brakes at all four wheels, heavy-duty suspension, white outlined Goodyear radial tires mounted to 15 x 7 front and 15 x 8 rear Rally wheels, distinctive Monte Carlo SS 454 markings, special paint, Hurst shifter, and plush interior. Are you ready

to turn the key and experience the heartbeat of today's Chevrolet?" That's the way a catalog should read! But alas, reality prevails, and this is only in my imagination—but no one said it couldn't be on your display shelf.

To build this sophisticated rodent you will need the following kits: Monogram's 1986 Chevy Monte Carlo SS no. 2731, 1970 Heavy Chevy Chevelle 3 'n 1 no. 2715, and the 1965 Vette Street Machine no. 2724.

I took the engine from the Chevelle kit and built right out of the box with the exception of the following: I took the manifold, carburetor, and air cleaner from

the Vette kit, and I had to trim the pipe for the exhaust manifolds from the manifold itself. I painted the block with Testor's Chevy engine orange and painted the intake manifold with aluminum. Next, I wired the engine. Using the Corvette shielding gives the engine a high-performance look and eliminates the need for a proper firing order, but if you want to use an exposed distributor, refer to the proper firing order diagram. I adapted belts and accessories from the Monte Carlo small block. In this fantasy it's the 1980s, so why not have air and power steering? I detailed the air cleaner with a Fred Cady engine displacement decal and painted the air cleaner element flat white. Then I set aside the entire assembly.

The chassis needed some minor massaging. I removed the original motor mounts and made my own using Plastruct angle plastic. Plastruct is strange in that it doesn't bond well unless you use Plastruct glue. I notched the front K member to accept the oil pan and starter. Then, by trial fittings, I modified

The driver's side chassis modifications are noted with arrows.

The passenger side chassis modifications are noted with arrows. Note exhaust manifold clearance, new motor mounts, and modified fan shroud.

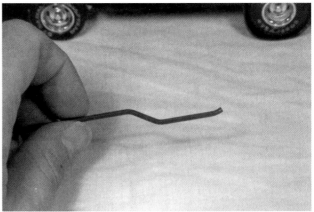

True duals are a must on any muscle car, so don't be shy with the knife!

I made new pipes from Auto World bendable rod.

the chassis rails to accept the width of the big block. Problem areas turned up near the exhaust manifolds on both sides. I also removed the lower fan shroud for clearance. On the underside, I made a slight indentation on the right side of the transmission cross member so that it would accept the second exhaust pipe. I painted the chassis in my usual manner, flat black with gloss black frame rails. The best way to do this is with a gloss black Tamiya paint pen—it's really quick.

Using the Monte's stock exhaust, I trimmed away the pipes in front of the mufflers, including the catalytic converter. I painted the remaining pipes

and mufflers with Monogram's Metalkote polished steel and buffed them after they dried. If you can't find this paint, Testor's Metallizer paints are an adequate substitute. With the engine taped to the chassis I finished the exhaust system using Auto World's bendable rod, saving the final gluing for later. I removed the plastic tailpipe extensions and added angle-cut 1/8″ aluminum tubing the same diameter as the plastic exhaust.

A high-performance Chevy must have a 12-bolt rear. I took one from AMT's 1971 Nova kit, but I liked the suspension setup on the stock Monte, so all I did was cut out both center sections and mate the 12-bolt section into

the Monte's axle tubes. This seems like a lot of fuss, but it looks great when you detail out the 12 little bolts.

I used the front tires from the Monte kit and made Rally wheels as described in Chapter 10. I cut trim rings from the Chevelle stock SS rims and mated them to MPC Rally centers. I made a stock offset for the front and a deep offset for the rear. To save time, you probably could use the Rally wheels that come in the Revell 1968 Vette kit. I took the larger rear tires from the Chevelle kit and detailed them to match the front set.

I modified the body in just two areas for engine fit: I notched a small area below the

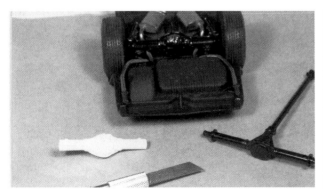

Chevys should have 12-bolt rears. I swapped the center section of the Monte Carlo for the 12-bolt unit.

I insisted on making my own deep offset Rally wheels.

I needed to notch the air conditioning unit molded to the engine compartment at the arrow for engine clearance.

The detailed interior shows a 1970s-type SS steering wheel, a four-speed shifter positioned in first gear, and—look closely at the ignition switch—that's right, scale keys on a key fob!

air conditioner fire wall unit, and I trimmed the fan shroud slightly. Then I epoxied the front and rear clips to the body. This makes the final assembly a bit tricky, but it eliminates gaps. I primed the body with Testor's camouflage gray and sprayed it with Testor's Model Master anthracite gray. I sanded the body after each coat of paint, which really brought out the shine. I should mention that I did the painting right out of the can. I used the LGM Micro Mesh polishing kit for sanding and polishing. If you haven't tried this yet, I encourage you to—it's easy to use, and the results are outstanding. Then I detailed the trim with flat black. I used Monte SS graphics from the Fred Cady sheet for a 1984 Monte, since these were my favorite graphics. I also used 454 badges from the Fred Cady Corvette sheet. Normally, I would overcoat the body with clear, but I was afraid I would ruin the beautiful finish. Instead, I waxed the body with Meguiar's Mirror Glaze no. 26 paste wax—what a finish!

Then I epoxied all the glass and the rearview mirror in place. The mirror mounts to the glass,

leaving just one shot at mounting it correctly. I used epoxy and waited until it was very tacky, then placed a drop of the glue on the mirror mount and positioned it on the inside of the windshield.

I basically built the interior stock with the exception of the four-speed shifter, pirated from the Chevelle kit. I removed the molded-on shift ball and replaced it with a black pinhead the same diameter. I detailed the boot and placed the unit in the opened area where the automatic shift went. I opened this area using an X-acto blade and files. I painted the interior red and overcoated it with semigloss, which gave the interior the right look. I also used the steering wheel from the Chevelle kit, since it was a vintage SS unit. As an added touch, I placed photoetched keys in the ignition. Each key has to be individually placed on a key ring, and they look real. They are available from S&S Specialties, and they are well worth the aggravation of assembly. I found that if you drill the hole in the keys slightly larger, they tend to fit the key ring better.

Next, I put together the subassemblies. I glued the interior into the body using epoxy so that I didn't distort the plastic at the mounting points. Then I slid the chassis into the body. Here's the tricky part: I left the engine loose in the chassis and, after the whole thing was positioned and together, glued it to the engine and transmission mounts. If you test-fit everything from the beginning, it should all fall right into place. Once this is completed, the exhaust system can be mated to the manifolds at the engine.

I backed the taillights with adhesive-backed foil to give them a reflective quality and depth. Final details included a radio antenna mounted on the fender, a "RAT" Illinois rear plate, and a "Heartbeat of America" front plate.

Just looking at the completed model with its big block and little keys in the ignition makes me start daydreaming. I can feel the keys in my hand making that big block come alive, hearing the exhaust rumble through unrestricted pipes. . . . I wonder if someone from Chevrolet is reading this?

18
BOULEVARD BRUISER
BUILDING A RESIN 1970 MONTE CARLO SS454

I never really took much notice of the 1970 Monte Carlo, since the car was predominantly classified as a "luxo-barge" back in the days of raw muscle. My cousin owned a forest green, 300 hp, 350-cubic-inch Monte with flat, color-keyed hubcaps. The car and its the hubcaps were totally unattractive to me at the time. My feeling about the car lasted for many years, until I attended a Super Chevy show and watched these luxo-barges turn some mighty impressive times on the track. My perception of the sophisticated Chevy changed. At that particular show, an entire row of cars was the SS454 version of the Monte Carlo, and my love affair with the car began. The classic sophistication had turned into raw power, reverberating through large exhausts and massive horsepower tucked under the hood.

Years later, while hunting for a parking space at work, I spotted a red 1970 Monte with its rear end high in the air and wide rubber tucked beneath it. I smiled, thinking this was a kid's car that was handed down over the years. As I approached the car I noticed the "MJ 454SS" license plate and thought, "Could this be a real SS?" The more I looked at the car, the more it became apparent that it was a real SS454. I don't recall exactly how the owner and I hooked up, but eventually we did meet, and somehow I got talked into building a replica of the car. In a few short weeks I had pictures in hand and a mission that

would take me more that a year and a half to complete.

1970 Monte Carlo Stats and Specifications

The 1970 Monte Carlo, designed by David Holls, was plagued by a strike at GM during the first days of production. The car debuted on September 18, 1969. It rode on a 116″ wheel base and had an expansive six-foot hood and heavy-duty shocks with an automatic leveling control system. It shared its wheel base with the Chevelle sedan and wagon. The Monte Carlo and Chevelle shared many other parts. The standard engine was a 350-cubic-inch small block, but my modeling focus is the SS454 version. Approximately 3823 SS units were built out of a total production run of 130,657 units. Out of the SS units produced, 100 were built with a four-speed transmission.

The Modelhaus had the complete kit I was looking for in resin. This was a natural resin progression for me, since I had only recently graduated to resin trans-kits. I first started with a few sporadic resin parts, soon moving on to trans-kits that use plastic kits as a donor for most of the conversion, now sliding into a complete resin buildup. My Modelhaus Monte came neatly packaged with a body, chassis, complete interior tub, drive line and exhaust system, complete chrome, and vacu-formed glass. This kit appeared to be a re-pop of the original Craftsman series 1970 Monte Carlo kit from AMT.

To begin the project, I subjected all nonplated resin pieces to a soaking in Westley's Blechewite white wall cleaner to remove mold release. I used a Rubbermaid plastic shoebox filled with Westley's Bleche-wite and let the body soak for a few days. You can see the effectiveness of the Westley's Bleche-white by the oily film that appears on the surface of the blue liquid after only a few hours.

Once the soak was completed, I washed the body and other parts in warm water with Dawn dishwashing liquid to remove any remaining residue. I heard that many dishwashing liquids now contain silicone, which will ruin your paint jobs by leaving "fish eyes"—areas where the paint does not stick to the surface.

While scrubbing the resin body I managed to snap the

Engines

Standard: 350 cubic inch,
    250 hp
Optional: 350 cubic inch,
    300 hp
    400 cubic inch, 265 hp
    400 cubic inch, 330 hp
    454 cubic inch (LS-4), 360 hp
    454 cubic inch (LS-5), 390 hp
    454 cubic inch (LS-6), 450 hp

Transmissions

Three-speed manual
Four-speed manual (M-20
    standard, M-21 optional)
Powerglide automatic
Turbo Hydro-matic

Colors and Codes

Classic White	10
Cortez Silver	14
Shadow Gray	17
Tuxedo Black	19
Astro Blue	25
Fathom Blue	28
Misty Turquoise	34
Green Mist	45
Forest Green	48
Gobi Beige	50
Champagne Gold	55
Autumn Gold	58
Desert Sand	63
Cranberry Red	75
Black Cherry	78

windshield pillar on the passenger side away from the body at the fender line. I decided to check my own original 1971 Monte Carlo kit and found that it too was broken in exactly the same spot. Apparently this is a weak spot in the kit, and naturally it would be a weak spot on the resin copy, so beware. I used a medium-grade Flexi-file for most of the body cleanup. The drive shaft was the most difficult to clean because of the roughness of the mold. I eventually put this aside and decided to scratchbuild a new one from $5/32''$ aluminum tubing and scrap box universal ends.

Just like the original, the resin body had fender skirts molded, which I needed to remove. This was easily accomplished with a no. 11 X-acto blade. Then I sanded the fender lips smooth. By removing the skirt, I needed to use wheel lip molding to finish off the wheel well and replicate the real car. Using Evergreen strip plastic no. 134, .030 x .080, and super glue, I carefully added the molding to the body. In places where it did not follow the contour, especially where the body tucks under, I trimmed the Evergreen strip. I used super glue to fill the gap between the molding and the

fender lip. Then I sanded the molding flat on top to give it distinctive prominence. This now matched the molding on the front fender well perfectly.

Since my replica needed a vinyl top, I needed to add molding to the roof. This molding was distinctive on a 1970 Monte Carlo, as it appeared to be a roof halo. This meant that the body color needed to show between the top of the windshield molding and the vinyl top molding. Body color was visible between the side drip rail molding and the top molding as well. This was difficult to recreate, but certainly not impossible. Using a mechanical pencil, I sketched the position of the molding onto the roof. Once I was happy with the shape and contour of the lines, I applied Evergreen strip no. 101, .010 x .030, around the entire circumference of the roof. It was easier to work with the Evergreen in short sections, tacking the strip with super glue as I went along, waiting for it to set, and then moving on. This method made tight bends easier to deal with. Patience here will really pay off—it took two sittings for me to complete the roof molding. Then I added two strips of Evergreen no. 100, .010 x .020,

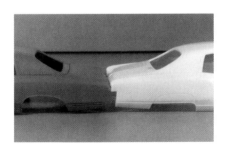

Here is the resin body after rear wheel well modification and with added roof trim (left) compared to an original, stock AMT Monte Carlo body (right).

The 1970 Monte Carlo had a distinctive, one-year-only, halo vinyl roof option. This picture is a front view of the vinyl top. You need to add the vinyl top seams prior to painting. Remember to carry the seams all the way to the trunk.

to the top of the roof to simulate the vinyl top seams. Be sure to use good references here, as they are invaluable. I flat-sanded all of the molding joints, which allowed for a more uniform appearance when I applied Bare Metal foil later. I used super glue to repair the broken windshield pillar.

Once all the glue had set, I washed the body to remove oils from handling. Then I scuff-sanded it using a 3200-grit sanding cloth from a polishing kit. This roughed up the surface enough to give the primer some bite into the surface, but did not leave deep sanding marks as a coarser grit might have done. Be warned that resin sands very easily, so you should check your work often and carefully.

From past resin experience I have learned to check the resin body for air bubbles. Air pockets can cause you major grief when sanding or filing resin parts. To check, all you need to do is hold the body up to a light bulb and look for thin spots. When working on the body, avoid these light spots if you can or build them up from behind with a mixture of super glue and baking soda. To Modelhaus' credit, my random purchased sample was free of any light spots or even any pin-holes. The piece actually worked easier than if it were a plastic kit. If you have never built a resin kit before, I urge you to spend the extra money and buy a quality kit. Too many times, first-time resin builders buy cheaper products with attractive prices, only to find problems when trying to assemble these bargains. Ultimately, these modelers never build a resin kit again. From past positive experience, my personal resin picks for trans kits or bodies are the following brands: The Modelhaus, All American Models, and Shawn Carpenter.

By no means should my word be taken as gospel. Talk to people who have built resin kits and ask them for their preferences, then formulate your own opinion about a product vendor.

When the Monte Carlo body was dry from its wash, I sprayed it with Plastikote lacquer primer no. 337. This normally is a very "hot" primer and can craze Styrene, but it's perfect for resins. I should note that the Evergreen plastic on the body was not affected by this primer. I set the body and hood aside for a few days to fully dry, then wet-sanded them with a 3200-grit sanding cloth, which revealed any imperfections. Normally a good automotive spot putty such as Evercote can be used for filling problem areas, but my project had no problems on the body or the hood. Again I washed the body, scrubbed it with a toothbrush, dried it, and reprimed it. To smooth out the final primer coat, I used a 6000-grit sanding cloth to sand the body, being careful not to sand through the primer coat. I again washed the body and set it aside to dry.

I easily cleaned up the chassis with a no. 11 X-acto blade and a medium-grit Flexi-file. I had originally planned to use the resin drive line and exhaust but the more I studied the real car, the more I leaned toward scratchbuilding these components—the original parts lacked the detail I was looking for. I painted the chassis with Testor's flat black, adding semigloss frame accents. I like to use this combination since most undercarriages on the East Coast I have had the pleasure to work under were undercoated. We rarely saw body color, and if we did, it was accompanied by a heavy dose of rust.

I had not decided what rear to use before I painted the chas-

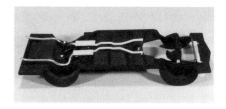

The resin chassis pieces were less than optimal. I scratchbuilt he rear suspension from the parts box and hand bent the tail pipes from aluminum tubing filled with solder.

sis. When I did decide, I realized that the axle locators molded on the chassis had to be removed. The real car I was replicating had its rear end way up in the air, and these axle locators would not allow for this height. Here is where I learned a valuable lesson. As I started to work with the chassis, I noticed that the paint was chipping away very easily. I also realized that primed surfaces did not chip as easily. Therefore, I would prime all my resin parts prior to color coats.

The resin differential was inadequate for my use—it didn't even look authentic. Remember, though, neither did the original kit. The plan was to use Otaki big and little tires on this replica, so I needed a differential that could take a large axle shaft through the axle tube. I found a 12-bolt differential center section in Revell's 1969 Yenko Camaro kit no. 7132. I cut off the kit axle tubes and drilled out the center section $5/32''$ to accept the same diameter piece of aluminum tubing. I drove this piece of aluminum tubing though the center differential section, cut it to the correct width, and then glued it to the center section. I used a set of parts box coil springs and modified lower control arms from a junk AMT 1970 Impala to fit the Monte chassis. The original exhaust was molded to the resin rear differential and had to

A Camaro center section, aluminum tubing, and lower control arms I found on a junker kit made up the rear end.

Once it all went together, it started to look good. Note how nicely the Otaki rear tires fit without any frame modification. I took rear shocks from Revell's 1969 Yenko Camaro kit.

be cut off from the mufflers back. I bent new tail pipes from 1/8˝ aluminum tubing filled with solder. This is a simple tube bending trick: Pick your tubing, slide a slightly smaller length of solder into it, and bend it to fit. On my project the driver's side bent up rather easily. Unfortunately, bending the passenger side pipe became quite a task. I bent up at least four sections of pipe before I achieved an acceptable fit. As easy as it was to bend the pipe, be aware that you only get one shot at bending the tube. If the bend is too complex, bending the tube back and reshaping it could cause a break. I notched the resin mufflers to accept the new tail pipes and super glued the rest of the system to the chassis. The completed rear drive line and suspension was now installed. I painted rear shocks from Revell's 1969 Yenko Camaro yellow and installed them.

The front suspension was generic and was only detail painted. I used front wheel spacers from F&F Resin Casting, as they gave the proper width spacing for the front wheels and tires. Trial-and-error is needed for exact fit, so take your time here. I adjusted the width spacing by thinning the axle locator. Once the chassis was completed, I added tires and wheels. I detail

painted the tires with white letters, then drilled the aluminum slotted wheels and fitted them with valve stems. Then I set this rolling assembly aside.

Returning to the body, I found the Cranberry Red paint on the Plastikote paint rack in an aerosol can, no. GM-7104. A Duplicolor substitute is no. GM-166. Then I masked the roof with Testor's Parafilm along the edge of the roof molding and sprayed the body with the Plastikote Cranberry Red. Once the body dried, I lightly polished it to remove any imbedded dust. After it fully cured, I overcoated the body with Model Car World's Nasclear top coat. I hung the body upside down and allowed it to dry for about a month. Once dry the body was a beautiful, deep glossy red. One mistake I made was to use a wire paint rack to hold the body. For some reason the pressure points on the inside of the body left faint spider web cracks in the urethane clear finish. Taping the body to the top of an aerosol paint can is a better alternative, or else bend the arms of your holder so that it doesn't exert so much pressure.

Once the body had dried and fully cured, I had a painted body and a primed roof. The vinyl top would still pose a problem, though. I have used stick-on tops

before, but found that over time the edges started to lift and left a rather unsightly model. I experimented with a few things and found the solution quite by accident—while looking through my paint rack, I accidentally tipped over a can of black wrinkle paint. I had nothing to lose, so I sprayed a scrap convertible top with the wrinkle paint. The sheen and texture were too much at first, but experimenting with topcoats of semigloss and flat finally gave me the look I desired. If you want an Armor-All look, overcoat the wrinkle paint with semigloss. If you want more of a service-use vinyl top look, spray the top with a flat overcoat. Now I masked the model in reverse, exposing only the roof, and applied Plastikote no. 217 black wrinkle paint. I used a no. 11 X-acto blade to free up the mask on the inside of the molding once the roof was painted. If the paint should chip in the process, a simple touch-up with flat black paint will mend the problem. Be sure not to get wrinkle paint up against the molding, as this will make foiling the molding difficult later.

Now is the time to apply Bare Metal to the body. For the fender SS 454 emblems, I used Woodland Scenics no. DT-575 dry transfer decals. I applied the letters to clear decal paper, trimmed them, and applied them at the proper location on the fender. This method was more manageable than trying to apply the individual letters to the rocker molding. I flowed flat black paint into the recess in the rocker molding and wiped away the excess. I painted the front marker lights with Tamiya clear orange no. X-26 and the rear markers with Tamiya clear red no. X-27. Since both sets of marker lights were in the rocker molding, which was chrome foiled, the clear colors had a good

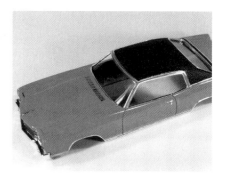

I detailed the engine with all kinds of goodies like AN fittings, collector flanges, high-tech wire looms, dual fuel line, prewired carb spring and bracket, and a throttle cable.

Note the photoreduced magazines, photo-etched cassettes, sunglasses, gauges, speakers, and pedals. The pink hat on the package shelf actually appears on the real car.

The body could be completely finished off the chassis and looked great alone.

reflective base. I easily trimmed out the vacu-formed glass and glued it into the body with white glue. Then I painted the entire inside of the body with flat black. I also added a rearview mirror to the inside roof of the interior. I set this entire assembly aside to dry completely.

The engine needed to replicate a hot street set up big block. I took the block from Revell's 1967 Chevelle kit no. 7147. Unfortunately it had a four-speed molded onto the block that I had to remove. I located a parts box automatic and grafted it onto the big block. The carburetor and air cleaner were also parts box additions. The headers proved to be a problem; they took quite a bit of time to locate and fit properly.

Eventually I used a set from AMT's 1971 Nova kit no. T-365. I thinned the head flange considerably and shortened the collector tubes, drilled them out, and added collector plates from Detail Master no. DM-2251. These headers were a nice fit and looked 100 percent better than the original ones. I used high-tech wire looms from Detail Resources, no. PWL-8, and added a Blue Moroso prewired distributor from Parts by Parks and care-

fully threaded it through the loom set. I have found it easier to open up the loom holes prior to threading the wire—this prevents the loom from stripping the insulation off the wire. I added Detail Master heater hose no. DM-1420 and radiator hose no. DM-1425 for additional realism. I located the engine in the chassis and tied in the exhaust system at this time.

I painted the interior with semigloss black and heavily detailed it using Detail Master custom pedals no. DM-2200, under-dash gauge cluster no. 2303, Detail Resources sunglasses no. PIJ-19, cassette tapes no. PIJ-19, rear speakers no. PDE-3, electric window switches no. PPS-45, and Scale Vanities photoreduced magazines. I flocked the carpet using Detail Master flocking no. DM-1609. I added a pink baseball cap just prior to assembly, to replicate an autographed hat given to the owner by "Cha-Cha" Muldowney. I took the hat from a figure I found in Revell's Truckers figure set no. 7440. I drew the autograph and hat design by hand using a no. 005 black and no. 005 red Micron Pigma pen.

Next, I put all the subassemblies and added the final details.

I detailed the engine compartment with an MSD box from Trae and Dad's no. TDM-05, a Detail Master coil DM-3052, and a paint-detailed battery. There was an unsightly gap between the fire wall and the cowl area that I filled with black Elmer's glue. This glue also works great in the glass area to simulate window sealant. I added a driver's door rearview mirror from Revell's 1969 Yenko Camaro kit no. 7132. I placed front and rear chrome in the appropriate locations. Be sure you do your trial-and-error fitting prior to painting, and remember to allow for paint thickness. Finally, I added touches such as the owner's own front and rear photoreduced license plates.

The completed model had the look and the feel of a muscular boulevard bruiser from the 1970s. Now came the hard part: parting with the model. The owner had only seen the assembly pictures of her replica but not pictures of the completed model. Remember, she still has not even seen the completed model! Hey, maybe she'll forget all about it and I could keep it. I know I'd certainly take good care of her boulevard bruiser!